The Love Of Money

DR. DEAN MELTON

FREEDOM CHRISTIAN CENTER
4020 FREEDOM DR.
CHARLOTTE, NC 28208
704-392-0137

DIAKONIA PUBLISHING
GREENSBORO, NORTH CAROLINA

THE LOVE OF MONEY
published by Diakonia Publishing

Copyright © 2007 by Dr. Dean Melton
ISBN: 978-0-9772483-7-7

Cover and book design by Jeff Pate

Unless otherwise noted, Scripture references and quotations were taken from THE HOLY BIBLE, Authorized King James Version, containing the Old and New Testaments. Published by Thomas Nelson, Inc. © Copyright 1970.

Scripture quotations are from Scripture quotations marked (NLT) are taken from the *Holy Bible*, **New Living Translation**, copyright © 1996. Used by permission of Tyndale House Publishers, Inc., Wheaton, Illinois 60189. All rights reserved.

No part of this publication may be reproduced, stored in a retrieval system, or transmitted, in any form or by any means—electronic, mechanical, photocopying, recording or otherwise—without prior written permission.

For information:
DIAKONIA PUBLISHING
P.O. Box 9512
Greensboro, NC 27429
www.ephesians412.net

Forewords

I first met Dr. Dean Melton in 1985, after moving to Mooresville, NC to pioneer a church in that city. A minister from Kannapolis introduced us that year at a monthly pastors' meeting at the Sheraton Hotel in Charlotte, NC.

Meeting Dr. Melton was an experience to say the least; he was not the typical preacher that you would expect to be in charge of a large group of ministers. There was no HYPE or SHOW about him; just a real person who loves people. At the same time there was a CHARISMA about him that could bring people together.

My family and I have been committed to him from that time on. He has been an inspiration to our family and church as he has imparted GODLY WISDOM to us over the years we have been under his leadership.

I have listened to him teach on many truths in the scriptures and found them to be so applicable, one of which is how to handle money. Dr. Melton is a gifted minister whom GOD has GRACED with an ability to teach and write, especially in the area of biblical finances.

His teaching on "THE LOVE OF MONEY" is practical and down to earth. As the scripture states in 1 Timothy 6:10, "the love of money is the root of all evil." Dr. Melton states that the love of money—not money itself—is the root of many evils, that money is

AMORAL being neither good nor evil. If used properly, money is good and godly; it is how and where you use it that determines its fruit.

I would recommend this book to be one of the BASICS to read; it can bring freedom to Christians in the area of how to handle money. In this book, you will hear the principles of the gospel put in practical form so that anyone can understand it.

Gary L. Kolstad, B. Min., M.B.S.
Senior Pastor
Freedom Christian Center, Inc.
757 Oak Ridge Farm Hwy.
Mooresville, NC 28115

Entering this world as an infant is an awesome experience common to us all. We all start out the same, knowing nothing. When we have grown enough to start wanting things, one of the first discoveries we all make about life is: if you want to possess things that you do not have, you have to have money. We begin by begging for pennies to get bubble gum, then dollars to get soft drinks, and the bigger dollars to go on dates, etc. The older we get, the bigger things we want, and the more money it takes to get them. It doesn't take long to discover that life on planet earth revolves around money.

Because of this, the Word of God tells us that the root of all evil is the love of money. Most have totally misunderstood this scripture and teach that money itself is evil. There in no intrinsic evil in money at all. As a matter of fact, it's next to impossible to exist in this world without it. It's the greedy, lustful, love of money that gives birth to all evil. Dr. Dean Melton give us a startling revelation about the love of money in this book that has the potential to set you free from financial bondages forever.

I have personally known Dr. Melton for more than twenty years, and consider him to be one of my closest friends. I have personally watched this man of God use a congregation of less than 250 members touch the world for Jesus with an impact, and do it debt free. They purchased land, and then built an entire city on it, including a huge church, medical clinic, schools, businesses, etc., drilled a deep well, built a water tower, and did it all DEBT FREE. They have similar works in the city of Manaqua, on the island of Ometepe, in the nation of Mexico in Acunia and Torreon. They also have thriving works expanding on the island of Cuba. While doing all of this, they have purchased eight acres on the west side of Charlotte, NC, established a church, a play school, senior ministries, etc. and they have done all of this with less than 250 members, no millionaires in the membership, and it's all DEBT FREE!

You might be thinking, "How is this possible?" They have used the principles Dr. Melton is about to teach you in this terrific book.

You are about to take an adventure in learning the truth about money, from which you will never want to return.

Harley W. Cline, D.Min., D.D.

When Dr. Melton told me he was having his teaching series from 1 Timothy 6:10, "The Love of Money" published, I became excited for the Body of Christ. As his teaching and understanding begins to circulate among the many members of Christ's Body, believers can finally get themselves into a financially secure and stable condition for their own personal lives, as well as enable them to fund and support their local church and its missions. This book, if read and acted upon diligently by those who will not "err from the faith" and who do not have "corrupt minds" and who are not "destitute of the truth" of Jesus Christ, will bring a tremendous outpouring of the Lord's supernatural financial anointing into every area of those individuals' lives!

Dr. Melton is my Apostle and as a son in the ministry and a local pastor for the past thirty years at Freedom Christian Center in Gastonia, North Carolina, I have heard this teaching often from the man of God's pulpit. But, just as important as it is to hear, the book of James says, "Faith without works is dead". I have watched over the years as Dr. Melton has put into practice the very principles and precepts of this teaching myself. I have watched him pour thousands of dollars into Freedom Ministries missions program: Ambassadors to the Nations. I've watched him give graciously to help other ministers and ministries. He lives by the principles of this book, and THE BOOK.

As a reshaped and refashioned United Methodist

pastor of fifteen years, who for the past fifteen years has pioneered a non-denominational ministry, my heart's desire is that I too will "owe no man nothing, except the love of God" and will become personally debt free; and that the ministry will also become debt free. And I know as I continue to apply these principles of God's Word in my personal life as well as in the Ministry—FINANCIAL FREEDOM & INCREASE are within my grasp! You too CAN prepare yourself for a journey into biblical truth utilizing the teaching in "The Love of Money!"

Barry E. Sullivan, B.A., M.Div.
President Freedom Christian Leadership University

Contents

1. God is Saving the Best for Last — 1
2. Don't Let Wealth Have You — 20
3. Money Is a Channel — 24
4. The Temptations of Wealth — 33
5. Put Your Money to Work — 57
6. God, Reveal Yourself to Me — 74
7. God is Shaking Things — 93
8. God Will Multiply Your Seed — 108

For the love of money is the root of all evil...
—1 Timothy 6:10

CHAPTER ONE

God is Saving the Best for Last

So the last shall be first, and the first last... —Matthew 20:16

I believe one of the greatest hindrances to people receiving the blessings of God is that they don't understand that God sometimes saves the best for last. People refuse to support something unless they get in at the beginning, thinking that this is best. I'm telling you that God makes the first last, and the last first. Can God not do what He wants to do? Does He have to have our permission to bless us? In Matthew 20:15 the master of the house said, *Is it not lawful for me to do what I will with mine own?*

In other words, he was saying, "Can't I do what I want to do with my own money?" God blesses who He wants to bless and if your heart is pure and right you might say, "God, I want to get in on something big." Like when our church was faced

THE LOVE OF MONEY

with paying off its mortgage, we all made commitments to pay $800 toward the debt until it was paid off.

This passage of Scripture means that God will bless you no matter what you give or do. I don't need a million dollars to be happy. If someone came and gave you a hundred thousand dollars you'd be grinning from ear to ear and you would think you had a million dollars, especially if it was in cash and you could look at it and know what it looked like. A cashier's check doesn't look like much but if you went to the bank and they handed you a hundred thousand dollars in bills, you are going to grin.

I am trying to challenge you. God knows how to take care of us. Listen to me, folks. I am not stupid. I am watching the economy. Things are not what they were a year ago. Every time you read something, somebody is down sizing. The Bible doesn't say that. Downsizing does not stop God from promoting you.

The Bible says that promotion comes from the Lord (Psalm 75:6-7). You will find favor with God and with man (Proverbs 3:4). Everything you touch shall prosper (Deuteronomy 28:8, 12). When you give, it will be given back to you (Luke

6:38). God said, I will open up the windows of heaven (Malachi 3:10).

God didn't say that when it gets tough I will tighten up my bowels in heaven. He didn't say that He couldn't pour you out blessings because the economy is slowing down. Instead, God says, "When you measure this out I will measure it back to you. Whatever you do, I will bring increase to it." God didn't say, "Wait a minute; let me look at the stock market a year before I make that decision." God is not moved by the stock market.

Jesus teaches this principle in Matthew 20:1-16: *For the kingdom of heaven is like unto a man that is a householder that went out early in the morning to hire laborers into his vineyard. And when he agreed with the laborers for a penny a day, he sent them into his vineyard. And he went out about the third hour and saw others standing idle in the marketplace. And he said to them, Go ye also into the vineyard and whatsoever is right I will give it to you.* [Matthew 20:1-4]

I want you to see that the householder went out in the morning and he hired laborers and he gave them a salary. He said, "I am going to pay you a certain amount of money." They went out and did the work. Three hours later he went out into the marketplace and he saw people standing by idly, doing nothing. He said, "Go into the vineyard and whatsoever is right, I will give it to you." They went their way. There was no agreement on money. He just said, "You go to work for me and I will take care of you."

Again he went out the sixth hour and the ninth hour and did likewise. And about the eleventh hour, he went out and found others standing by idle. He said unto them, Why stand ye here all day idle? They said to him, Because no man has hired us. [vv. 5-7]

Listen to me, folks. I am telling you what God will do if you will just get involved with what God is doing. These people said, "We are not going to work because there was no one that came out here and hired us. We don't have a job. We have no ability to make money, so we are standing here idly."

A man comes by and says, "Listen, I am about ready to bless you all." God said you should quit struggling and just get involved. Find the place where you can get involved. To a Rockefeller or a Kennedy a million dollars isn't much. But to you it would be. However, you could give a few hundred or even a thousand dollars. I am not asking you to give a million dollars. I am telling you to find your place.

In this parable, the eleventh hour came and the man went out and found others standing idle, and he said to them, "Why stand here all day long?" They said, "Because no man has hired us." In other words, "No man has told us the truth. Nobody has spoken to us." He said unto them, "Go ye also to the vineyard and whatsoever is right, that shall you receive."

So when evening was come, the lord of the vineyard said to the steward, Call the laborers and give them their hire beginning with the last unto the first. [v. 8]

Look what he said there. "When you go out, don't go to the ones you hired first, but go to the ones you hired last." When they that were hired about the eleventh hour they received every one of them a day's wages but when the first came they should have received more.

This is a great teaching on the equality of God's grace, whether you get in at the beginning or at the eleventh hour. God's blessing is still the same and this parable teaches that those who come into the kingdom last will receive first. And sometimes what comes last is better than what comes first as

Saving the Best For Last

In John 2, the Lord had been invited to a wedding feast and during the feast, they ran out of wine. Jesus' mother said to the servants, *Whatever he says to you, do it. And there sat six water pots of stone after the manner of purifying of the Jews, containing two or three firkins apiece. Jesus said unto them, Fill the water pots with water. And they filled them up to the brim. And he said unto them, Draw out now and bear unto the governor of the feast, and they bore it. When the ruler of the feast had tasted the water that was made wine and they knew not whence it was (but the servants that drew the water knew;) the governor of the feast called the bridegroom, and he said, Every man at the beginning does set forth good wine; and when men have well drunk then that which is worse, but thou has kept the good wine until now.* [John 2:5-10]

What if God had held it all back until this moment to dump it on us? During the time we were trying to pay off the church, what if God had just wanted to find out if we had enough fortitude, or guts inside of us and we proved to God that in seven months we were going to pay the church off?

The Bible says, "You saved the best until the last." *This beginning of miracles did Jesus in Cana of Galilee and manifested forth his glory and his disciples believed in him.* [John 2:11] Isn't that good news? This is the beginning of miracles. What if this is the beginning of blessings like you have never seen before?

What if God said, "Because you have taken care of My house, I am going to start taking care of your house." Because of what you have done for God, He is going to prove to you that He's not el-cheapo. What if God is the "breasted one" and has more than enough milk for you all?

Mary said, "Whatever my son tells you to do, you do it."

Now He said, "Go, pour water."

That is not wine, folks. That's water and can you imagine if they had tasted water that day instead of wine? They would have probably all lost their lives. I am telling you, by the authority of God's word that we haven't even tasted of the good wine yet. The Bible says that the wealth of the sinner has been laid up for the just (Proverbs 13:22). God said, "Everything you touch is going to prosper. Whatever you put your hands to I am going to bring increase to it." Has that day happened yet in your life?

If I could guarantee you a hundredfold return off of everything you give, you would give it. I have been doing this now for almost thirty years and sometimes I tell God to just give me back what I gave to my congregation. Can you imagine what a hundredfold return would mean to you? If God just brought a hundredfold return on everything you've given, you couldn't hold it all in your automobiles. A light estimate of how much I have put in my church over the last twenty years would probably be somewhere around a half a million dollars. My God, if you multiplied that times a hundred!

Some of you might say, "Brother, I don't think God wants to do that."

Well, I say if Isaac was blessed like that and he didn't have anything, what would God do for us? If we would just believe it to be so, then we would see it!

I am telling you that this is the beginning of miracles for you. God said it doesn't make any difference when you started work—only that you started. Can you imagine somewhere along the line that Jesus is going to come back – let's say He comes back in one more year? You know there are some people that will come and get born again during the last week. There will be some people that will hear the word of God and be like I was at the first sermon I heard back in February 1972, when I reached down in my pocket and put my last $90 into the collection plate. I walked out of that church broke, but I have never been broke since. Someone is going to do the same thing—take everything out of their pockets and put it in the offering plate and walk out of that church and be a millionaire in less than a week. There will be some of us that could get jealous.

When God gets ready to release the wealth of the sinner, it is going to fall on everyone who is just. He didn't say this applied to those who've been Christians for thirty years. He simply said it falls on the just. Do you hear what I'm saying? It won't look fair. Folks, it's not fair – it is just. We have found out that it doesn't make a difference what hour you get in on it as long as you get in on it. Jesus said that the last ones will be made first. That's good news!

The Lord taught the same thing in the parable of the prodigal son (Luke 15:11-32). The brother had remained with his father all the time and the father said that everything he had belonged to him. He could have eaten all the fat cows he wanted. The brother was angry because the prodigal son came home and they killed one for him. But the father said, "You had them all the time. You had the inheritance anytime you wanted it. The blessings of God have always been at your doorstep."

When He turned the water to wine, we see that Jesus wanted to begin the outpouring of His blessings. It was like He said, "Listen to Me. I want to start miracles. I want to begin the blessings." Somewhere in our lives, God has to start it. *This beginning of miracles did Jesus in Cana of Galilee and manifested forth his glory and his disciples believed in him.* This passage means that up to this point there had been no miracles, but from that point on, miracles started in this man's life. For three and a half years He walked in the miracles of God. How would you like to start this month as the next three and a half years of your life? At the end of that time the rapture comes and Jesus takes you out—not as a weak, anemic human being, but full of the power of God. All the wrinkles, blemishes and spots will no longer operate in your life. You have overcome. There is a point that Jesus is going to start to finish up what He is about to do. I feel like the hour is getting close. This could be the hour – God has to find somebody to start working through Him. He has looked through all eternity to find someone who will just believe. Why shouldn't you be that believer? Why don't you become part of who God has been looking for all these years to begin the last days? Don't get jealous if somebody comes in here at the last minute. I rejoice with them.

Matthew 18:23-27 says, *The kingdom of heaven is likened unto a certain king which would take account of his servants and when he began to reckon one was brought unto him which owed him ten thousand talents but for as much as he had not paid him, his lord commanded him to be sold and his wife and children and all that he had and the payment be made and the servant therefore fell down and worshipped him and said, Lord, have patience with me and I will repay you. Then the lord of the servant was moved with compassion and loosened him and forgave him of his debts.*

This man was forgiven of his indebtedness; yet when he had an opportunity to take care of

THE LOVE OF MONEY

someone else, he didn't do it. *But the same servant went out and found one of his fellow servants, which owed him one hundred pence, and he laid hands on him and took him by the throat and said, Pay me what you owe. And his fellowservant fell down at his feet and besought him, saying, Have patience with me and I will pay you all. And he would not; but went out and cast him into prison until he could pay the debt. So when his fellowservants saw what was done, they were very sorry and came and told their lord all that was done. Then his lord, after he called him said to him, You wicked servant. I forgave you all your debts because you desired me. Should you not also have had compassion on your fellowservant, even as I had pity on you? And his lord was wroth, and delivered him to the tormentors until he should pay all that was due him. So, likewise shall my heavenly Father do also unto you, if you from your heart forgive not every one his brother their trespasses.* [vv. 28-35]

If you can't take care of someone else, how can God take care of you? When we were raising money to pay off the church's debt, I took care of a few people's money. Part of the reward for keeping their vow was that I would take them out for a steak dinner. I made sure they gave their money properly so they would be blessed. One man was earning $7.00 an hour and worked less then thirty hours a week. He was tithing to everything we did. He had already met his vow and he had paid $1450 to go to Nicaragua for a mission trip. This man had $700 in give-away money to take with him and still had thousands of dollars in the bank. I wanted to make sure he would be blessed with all of us.

God said, "I have forgiven you, why don't you help others?" In Matthew 19:23-24, Jesus said unto his disciples, *Verily I say unto you a rich man shall not hardly enter into the kingdom of heaven. Again, I say it is easier for a camel to go through the eye of a needle than it is for a rich man to enter into the kingdom of God.*

Everyone that has forsaken houses, brothers, sisters, husbands, wives and children and land for Jesus' namesake, you shall receive full return *and* everlasting life. It is emphatic. If you do what the word of God says, God said, "I will multiply it a hundredfold."

Some people say, "I am not into all that giving and getting back."

THE LOVE OF MONEY

If you don't allow God to do that, then you make yourself to be higher than God. When you tell God, "God, I am not looking for you to bless me, God, I don't want you to give me anything back", you make yourself to become God. Look what he said. *Every one of you that have forsaken houses, brothers, sisters, or father or mother, or wife or children and land for my namesake shall receive a hundred-fold return.* [Matthew 19:29]

Notice the Lord said, "If you do this I SHALL multiply a hundred-fold return back into your life and you shall also have everlasting life, but many that are first shall be last and the last shall be first."

If I have a million dollars and you have ten million dollars I am going to shout with you. I'll be honest with you – I would have a hard time spending a million dollars! I am not going to be jealous because you have ten million, because if I use that million properly and do what's right with God, I will have ten million dollars in a few months. I am challenging some of you. Don't worry when someone comes on board late in the game. God will bless you accordingly. God will take care of them and He will take care of you.

Remember what the passage from John 2 says: "The best for last". You are going to get the best of God for yourself. Remember this. This was the start of blessings. When you predetermine to do what God tells you to do, it will turn things around in your life. Most people don't turn it around because they never make a decision. Try it. If it doesn't work, quit.

One of our missionaries to a foreign country couldn't go down there and make $500-$600 a week working a job. He knows he has to do what God puts in his heart because you can't go down there and make any money. If that were true, there wouldn't be foreigners coming to America. If they were paying them more money, they would want to stay there. I told this missionary, "When you come, we want to show you we appreciate what you are doing. We appreciate that you are doing missionary work."

This man gave up his life and God says when you give up your life, I will take care of you. If I take care of Him, what is God going to do for me? If I make sure I minister something for Him, what is God going to do for my life?

The principle taught in Matthew 18:23–35 is that God will treat you the way you treat others. God was telling me if you take care of someone else, I will take care of you. Do you hear what I am saying? I don't care what the economy does. I don't care how many jobs go down the toilet. The Bible says, "It will not come near your dwelling place" (Psalm 91:10) .

If your heart is right before God, increase is coming. By giving, you can double your paycheck before the end of this year. Matthew 23:19-30 says that if you are blessed, you should bless others. People worry about how they are going to get to heaven and God says, "I am going to take care of you and give you eternal life."

I have eternal life. I am not going to heaven; I am living in heaven right now. Do you hear what I am saying? Some of you may say, "Well, brother, I know, but you are not really in heaven."

The Bible says I am living in heavenly places in Christ Jesus (Ephesians 2:6). The Bible says I am living far above this earth. This earth has no pull on my life. God is not involved in this economy. God is up there looking down at me. As far as God is concerned, He has already elevated us up to where He is. If He has elevated me, He knows exactly what is going to happen next month, and He has already made a way of escape for me. He has said, "Come up here and see what I have done for you. When they are closing everything else down, look how I am promoting you."

Some people ask me, "How do you do all you do and the people in your church are not broke?"

I answer, "God opens up the windows of heaven. God brings promotion. Folks, if you don't get sick, you don't need medicine. If you don't go to a hospital, you don't need doctors. If you don't die, you won't need a funeral or a plot. I have to prepare for the future. You are going to live for a long, long time around here. The angels of the Lord are camped about those who fear God (Psalm 34:7). God said if you honor your mother and father I will make your days long on this earth (Exodus 20:12). Are you listening to me? I am giving you a covenant. In Genesis 6:3 the Lord said, "I am giving you 120 years." Are you listening to me? He is a God of abundance. He will give you all you want. You don't have to die, folks. You can wait on Jesus to come back.

These are the days of Elijah and then we begin to sing how He is coming back and when He is coming back. He is coming back for us! He is not coming back for Mormons, Buddhists, etc. He is coming back for believers—those who are looking for His appearance and I don't need a graveyard site to let me see Him. I am trying to chal-

THE LOVE OF MONEY

lenge some of you. I want to hang around here for a while.

I see kids today that die. I recently saw on the news where two kids were riding down the road too fast and spun around and flipped over and went down an embankment. People say, "I don't understand." The serpent can't bite unless their hedges are down. You don't hear what I am saying – Satan can't kill anybody unless the hedge is down. When the hedge comes down, Satan comes in and bites and devours. Thank God the hedge is up.

God has delivered me from car wrecks. When I was sixteen years old, I used to go over to a racetrack and we'd race our cars. I had a 1962 Ford and another boy had a 1955 Chevy. One night we went over there and marked off a quarter mile. During the race, I looked at my speedometer and when I hit fourth gear I was doing 120 miles an hour. At that time, I realized we had gone too far beyond the point and I remembered there was a sixty foot drop off the road. When we approached the drop, I began downshifting to third gear, second gear, and I knew I was going over that cliff. I just turned it sideways and spun in the road. When I came to a stop, I knew right then and there that only by the grace of God was I alive. If I had gone over that embankment, I wouldn't be preaching today. I would be in heaven right now. Thank God we are protected.

God said this to me, "There are some I am sending in during the last hour – don't get jealous when I bless them. When they get connected with what we are doing, don't get all bent out of shape because I poured out in the last few days what it took you twenty years to get. Just remember, it was My money. It is Mine and I will take care of any of those that get in here at the last minute just like I have taken care of you for the whole forty years of your Christianity."

Listen to me, folks. Don't get jealous if someone hooks into this blessing. Rejoice and shout with them! I am challenging some of you. I am telling you that this is your year. Mine is coming in any day now. God says, "I know how to take care of my people."

God is saving the best for the last.

CHAPTER TWO

Don't Let Wealth Have You

No man can serve two masters. For either he will hate the one, and love the other; or else he will hold to the one, and despise the other. You cannot serve God and money. —Matthew 6:24

When Jesus spoke these words, He was telling us who we are to serve, and what is to be our servant. If we have God to be our Master, then money cannot be our master. Therefore, if God is our Master, then money is our servant to work His righteousness in the world.

Unfortunately, most people, although they understand this teaching, don't apply it properly. They don't have wealth or money. Rather, wealth has them under its control. Money determines whether they are happy or sad. What do you do to get money? Do you lie, cheat or steal to get money? Would you do anything to line your pockets with money, knowing that all that stuff is wrong? Would you cheat or steal, or kill someone? There are people every day who do that for money. If you get too much money and you aren't able to handle it or control it, that money will control you and it will destroy you. This is the truth. Some of you make $400 - $500 a week and you are in bondage to money.

Repeat these words: "Jesus, I am making decisions today. Not just to be safe, but my whole life and my destiny is in the power of my tongue. The way I perceive and the way I speak determines my destiny. Satan has no authority over me. Satan has no power over me. He is not a Lord over me. Father, You have given me that power. You have given me that authority. You don't want to make all the decisions for me. You want me to make righteous decisions. That's the reason you said, "Power and authority I give unto you."

I have received that power and authority. I believe it is God's ability, God's life; it is who God is, and I am trying to operate like Jesus would operate. When Jesus saw hungry people, He fed them. When He saw that taxes needed to be paid, He paid them. That means He did everything that was righteous. Jesus said, "Render unto Caesar what is Caesar's and unto God what is God's." God, this is the way we are going to live.

THE LOVE OF MONEY

Some of our more modern Bible translations use the word "servant" instead of the true meaning of the word, which is actually "slave." A lot of people in America would get offended at the word "slave" but the Bible says that when you work for your employer, your employer becomes your master and you become his slave. The Bible tells you how to serve your employer; and it also tells the employer how to treat his servants or slaves. Unfortunately, most employers don't know how to take care of their people; and because money is to be your servant, most people don't know how to take care of it.

Money is only a tool in your hands to bless, to work the righteousness of God in this world. The Lord through the prophet Malachi said, I will open up the windows of heaven and pour out a blessing, that there shall not be room enough to receive it (Malachi 3:10).

We should be expecting that to happen right now. If we view money as our servant—as a tool to be used to benefit the kingdom of God, we can experience the overflowing blessing of God promised in Malachi. There's an old saying, "If God can get it *through* you, He'll get it to you."

There are some of you right now that God has

given you an idea and a dream and you thought it would never happen. I am telling you that dreams and inventions are going to start flowing out of us like rivers of living water. You are not going to work for companies – you will *own* companies. You are not just going to get by – you are going to treat your employees with respect and kindness and you will love those that serve you and will give to those that help you, because God said He can trust you today.

Lord I don't want wealth to control me. I want to control wealth. I just want to be a channel for you in these last days. Let us be the Father to children – let us show them what it is to be an example. Let us be the carbon copy that others would want to copy. Let them come to us and say, "We want to pattern our church after what you are doing because we know God has blessed you."

CHAPTER THREE

Money Is A Channel

But godliness with contentment is great gain. —1 Timothy 6:6

Godliness with sufficient blessings of food and clothing should make one content with life. If God is taking care of your needs, you should be so contented now with what God gave you that you don't know what you are going to do with it.

All some people want is a handout – gimme, gimme, free! The Bible says that if something doesn't cost you anything – you won't appreciate it.

We brought nothing into this world and it is certain we won't carry anything out. When you came out of your Momma's womb you were a mess. Thank God someone was there to clean you up. You sure didn't look very good when you came out, so Paul reminds Timothy, "You brought nothing into this world and it is certain you won't carry anything out and having food and raiment, let us therefore be content." You don't have to keep up with others – not the Kennedy's nor the Rockefellers.

Contentment is knowing that God has provided your basic needs according to His riches in glory by Christ Jesus (Philippians 4:19). I don't keep up with anybody. I just want God to bless me. If He blesses me, I will have enough to take care of me, my wife and all the needs in my life.

Our church has been blessed with a prosperity that baffles others in Charlotte. You know why? Because we are contented. We are not in a contest. The Bible says, *Having brought nothing in, having food and raiment, let us be therewith content.* [1 Timothy 6:7-8]

It also says, *But they that will be rich fall into temptation and a snare, and into many foolish and hurtful lusts, which drown men and destruction and perdition.* [v. 9] When your motives are not right, money can absolutely bring you down to your knees, for the *love of money* is the root of all evil. *The love of money.* It didn't say *money* – it says the "love" of money. I love money! I love to smell it – I love to spend it – I love to buy things with it. Most of all, I love to give it away. You know what? People say, "My God, you are crazy." There are people who would kill someone for $200. People would shoot somebody for a lousy twenty bucks.

It says right here – for the love OF money. Money is not bad. It is the love OF money. What would you do to get it? Would you steal from me, rob me, cheat me? There are thousands of dollars that come into my church every week. If I were to go back and steal that money because I want a big car and a big house – that's the love of money. I would let my congregation struggle to get by, but I would go live in a big house and drive a fine car. Then they try to get by on $15,000 - $18,000 a year while I take $200,000 out of the church and live like a king. That's the love OF money! The Scripture says, *For the love OF money is the root of all evil, which while some coveted after, they have erred from the faith and pierced themselves through with many sorrows.* [1 Timothy 6:10]

People argue over the dumbest things. God is able to you everything back, and you argue over whether I give tithes of $400 or $300? If someone gives me $100 do I tithe on it? Keep the money. You need it. People argue over a $10 gift to God? When He will give you a hundred times back? When money holds you in bondage, you can be destroyed by it.

That's the love OF money. Paul then urges Timothy, *But thou, O man of God, flee these things...* [v. 11] Flee from what things? The things you just read above – the love OF money! He's talking about coveting money.

Let money be a channel for you to do something. Do you hear what I am saying? My God, get a dump truck full of it. Fill the building full of $100 bills. I don't care, but does that mean you can't have a brand new Mercedes or a house on the lake? Have a hundred homes. God doesn't care. But, when God puts something before you as a Christian – to support His kingdom – does that freak you out? If it does, then you know that you are in bondage.

When we were in Nicaragua a few years ago, we visited a man and his wife and ten children. We had bags of beans, rice, flour and tortillas and the man fell to his knees and cried out and said, "We were in a circle saying, 'Lord, we have no food – God we are depending on you – God do you care about us?'" God cared! I never forgot that.

He wept like a child. I will never forget it.

Paul continues to say, *But, thou, O man of God, flee these things and follow after righteousness and godliness, faith, love, patience. Fight the good fight of faith...*

What does he want you to fight? The love OF money. Don't let money control you.

...lay hold onto eternal life when thou art also called, and hast professed a good profession before many witnesses. I give thee charge in the sight of God who quickeneth all things, and before Christ Jesus, who before Pontius Pilate witnessed a good confession. [vv. 12-13]

People who know me know that I am not a tightwad. We joke because I don't waste money. I will save a dollar to give it away. We go look for something on sale to save five dollars and the reason we do that is that gives me five dollars to sow into the Kingdom. Most people, when they go out to dinner, order a large drink with their meal. Do you know what I order? I order a small drink and that gives me eighty cents saved to sow. Multiply that by 365 days and you have saved $250!

The Bible says in 1 Timothy 6:17-21, *Charge them that are rich in this world that they be not high minded.* Do you understand what that is talking about? Paul wrote before that the love OF money is the root of all evil. Money will pull you off your faith. If money is what you want, then you will start coveting another man's property; and before long you are doing things wrong instead of fighting the good fight of faith. Seek out the righteousness and godliness and faith, love, patience and meekness – do these things. Let people know why you live your lifestyle.

Paul continues, *Charge them that are rich in this world that they be not high minded nor trust in uncertain riches but in the living God who giveth us richly all things to enjoy.* Does that mean I can have a boat? Have five of them! Does that mean I can have a car? Have the best car in town. Why drive around in just a car when you would like to have a Rolls Royce. Get a Rolls – I don't care, but when you're asked to put a dollar in the offering plate don't freak out! It's like your whole life is coming apart. A dollar should be nothing more than chump change to some of you out there.

Paul continues in verses 18-19, *That they do good, that they be rich in good works, ready to distribute, willingly to communicate, laying up in store for themselves a good foundation against a time to come that they may lay hold on eternal life.*

That passage does not talk about going to heaven. It means that by giving to others, you can expect a return to draw upon in your time of need. How do you draw on that? You stand on the word of God by confessing your covenant.

This is what should be coming from your mouth: "Father I thank you. I have been bringing tithes and offerings to the house of God. I want to thank you that your word says you will open up the windows of heaven and you will bless my life. Father, right now I thank you that I have everything I need. Father, I want to thank you that you said I can draw on the power of your word that says that I have eternal life and that I have the ability to draw from you. God, I need it right now."

Tired of living in the little cracker box house you live in? Draw on it – stand on God's word and do something. Go build someone else a house and get yourself a hundred houses. The Bible says that whatever a man soweth so shall he reap in this life (Galatians 6:7).

God is telling you right here in 1 Timothy, *That they do good, that they be rich in good works, ready to distribute willingly to communicate, laying up in store for themselves a good foundation against the times to come, that they may lay hold on eternal life.*

Can you not see that? Paul closes his letter by saying, *O Timothy, keep that which is committed to thy trust, avoiding profane and vain babblings, and oppositions of science falsely so-called.* [v. 20]

Some of you may say, "Brother, I am not into all that prosperity teaching."

I say, "Then stay poor and leave me alone! Make yourself into a new-age person, then. You believe that you are God. You are telling me that your God is not able to minister back to you greater than you minister to Him."

People say, "I know that Dean over there – that preacher – he is into all that faith stuff."

Well thank God I live by faith. Thank you, God.

I challenge you to trust God's word. When I give to the poor, God said, "You are lending to me." Is there anything you can't lend to God? Can you imagine how God pays you back? Even to a hundred fold return. Some of you haven't hooked into the hundred fold return yet. Most of you approach giving by wadding up your money and throwing it in the offering plate. You wouldn't plant seeds like that in your garden. If you went out in the yard and planted flowers or vegetables, you would be very specific. How is it then that you come up and throw your money and act like you did God a favor?

Don't let money rule you. If you control money, then you can be a channel for the outpouring of God's blessing.

CHAPTER FOUR

The Temptations of Wealth

That night God appeared to Solomon in a dream and said, "What do you want? Ask, and I will give it to you!" —2 Chronicles 1:7 [NLT]

I love money! Some of you might say, "You can't say that! The Bible says, 'Money is the root of all evil.'" They didn't understand what it said. The Bible says, *The love OF money is the root of all evil.* [1 Timothy 6:10] The emphasis is not on the word "money." Money is not the evil – it is the love OF money that is wrong.

While studying the scriptures, I began to find out that if you get too much money and you aren't able to handle it or control it, that money will control you and it will destroy you. That is a proven fact. Some of you make $400 - $500 a week and you are in bondage to money. There are people that make $500 a week and wouldn't give God $50 a week but yet the Bible tells you that you are to honor God with the firstfruits of your increase

THE LOVE OF MONEY

(Proverbs 3:9).

Only through the word of God will you find out that God wants you to have money – bucket loads of it – truck loads of it. He wants you to have gold and silver. He wants you to have so much you can't even spend it all. You'll have to give it away. But, if you can't be faithful over a few hundred dollars a month, or a few thousand, how could God ever trust you with millions? We are confessing the wealth of the sinners, but we fuss over the net or the gross. If God blesses you with something, you fight over how much you should give. I found out why most people are in bondage. It is because that's what they seek after – money. You shouldn't have to seek after money. Money should be seeking after you. Money should be knocking your door down trying to get into your back pockets because you are a channel for God.

The Bible says that you were born naked and you will leave this earth naked (Job 1:21). That means between nakedness and nakedness you have to make a decision. You will determine your own destiny from the time you are born to the time you are 120 years old. You are the one to make decisions on what you are going to do with

THE TEMPTATIONS OF WEALTH

your life; and you can have a heart for God and for the things of God. When you're faced with the opportunity to give, how do you respond to those things? Do you say, "Jesus, they are after all my money"? Or, do you say, "They are after me to sow everywhere"?

Solomon is a great example of a person who had a heart for God and made right decisions. The Bible says, *That night, God appeared to Solomon in a dream and said 'What do you want? Ask and I will give you.'* [2 Chronicles 1:7 NLT] Some of you don't realize that God wants to give you the desires of your heart. Most people are getting their desires but most of your desires are so modest and that's why you are having such a hard time holding on to what you have. The Bible talks about it. You have a bag with a hole in it. You have plenty, but it is never enough. It looks like you are full, but you are always empty (Proverbs 11:24).

God has blessed you. He is giving you $300, $500, $800 a week. You have a house, a car, but they are always causing you problems. Your car is always broken down; your clothes are always wearing out and it seems like every day you have to go to a doctor or dentist. It seems like the more money you make the more it takes. How would you like to make a lot and not owe anybody anything? How would you like to never get sick and not have to go to a doctor? How would you like not to have to take medicine anymore? How would you like to have more than enough?

God came to Solomon that night and said, "What do you want from me – ask." That is an emphatic question right there. It was like God was saying, "You can ask for anything at this moment and I will give it to you." You know, Solomon could have said, "I want a million dollars." God would have given it to him. Then he could have said, "I want a hundred wives." God would have said, "They are yours." God said, "Ask me anything and I will give it to you."

We are living way below our covenant today. We tell the Lord, "Just give me a little cabin in Glory. Lord, when I get there if I just have a little mud hut."

You don't want a little mud hut in Glory. Be honest! You want a Jacuzzi with water jets; you want a big bathtub, a nice big room. You don't want to walk into the closet and bump into your furniture and lie down on your little twin bed! You want nice things but yet you think it sounds religious if you just tell God, "Just give me a little" You know what? God says, "I will give you that little cabin in Glory. You are living in it right now."

How many people know that they are living in Glory right now? I promise when you get to Heaven there are no little mud huts or log cabins in Heaven. Jesus is a skilled craftsman. If He were building a house it would be the best one in town. You get the biggest one – not the smallest one!

Solomon replied to God, *You have been so faithful and kind to my father, David, and now have you made me king in this place. Now, Lord God please keep your promise to David, my father, for you have made me king over people as numerous as the dust of the earth. Give me wisdom and knowledge to rule them properly, for who is able to govern this great nation of yours.* [vv. 8-10]

God said to Solomon, *Because your greatest desire is to help your people.* You should commit this to memory! He said, "Solomon, because your greatest desire is to help your people." Solomon didn't con God. If your heart is not right, God knows. That's the reason you stumble and fall and struggle every day of your life. How do you change what is in your heart? You say, "God, I want to become different. God, train me, teach me, show me your way." All of a sudden things begin to change and things don't look the same. Things you used to like, you now hate. All of a sudden things that you didn't care about, you fall in love with.

All of a sudden, God looks at Solomon and says, *Because your greatest desire is to help your people, you have not asked for a personal wealth, an honor, or death to your enemies, or even long life, but rather you have asked for wisdom and knowledge to properly govern my people and I will certainly give you the wisdom and knowledge that you requested. I will also give you riches and wealth and honor such as no other king has ever had before you or will again ever have.* [vv. 11-12]

You know what I want? One dollar less than what Solomon had. The Lord said, "There will be nobody that will ever have what you have, Solomon. You will have it all." I don't covet what Solomon had; I just want a dollar less than what he had. Now if I have a dollar less than what Solomon had, you can't ask for what I have. God says you can't do that. You can't have another man's wife, you can't have another man's dream.

THE TEMPTATIONS OF WEALTH

I don't desire Solomon's wealth. I have my own dreams.

I want to take care of God's people. I want to build schools and colleges. Maybe one day I want to own a motel and have a home for the elderly. They can have a place where they can go and stay and we take care of them and have a fine restaurant they can eat in and we don't have to charge them $2,000 a week! If I got Solomon's wealth less a dollar, I can promise you, folks, I can do all that and won't have to charge for it.

If you had a dollar less than Solomon, you would never have to worry about money the rest of your life, folks. The Bible said that people came from great distances to see the wisdom of Solomon (1 Kings 4:34).

How would you like people to knock on your door and say, "The Lord told me to bring you another million." Then the next day there is another million, and the next another one and another one. For the next 365 days, everyone brings you another million and you say, "I have all I can stand." But God says, "No, I am going to bless you beyond measure."

That's what they did to Solomon. The way you will get this is not asking for your Cadillac and your big homes. You are going to get it when you say, "God, let me help somebody else. Let me help other people. Let me be a blessing God. Give me wisdom on how to treat other people."

God said, "Because you asked that, I will give you everything else everyone seeks for but I will give it to you." I want to have part of that covenant – don't you? I want to be part of a covenant that will bless me beyond measure, that even wealthy people will search me out.

Solomon said, "God, give me wisdom to rule your people." God said, "Fine, Solomon, I am going to honor you with riches and wealth such as no other man had before or after you."

Then Solomon returned to Jerusalem from the Tabernacle at the hill of Gibeon, and he reigned over Israel. Solomon built up a huge military force, which included fourteen hundred chariots and twelve thousand horses. He stationed many of them in the chariot cities, and some near him in Jerusalem. During Solomon's reign, silver and gold were as plentiful in Jerusalem as stones. And valuable cedarwood was as common as the sycamore wood that grows in the foothills of Judah. Solomon's horses were imported from Egypt and from Cilicia; the king's traders acquired them from Cilicia at the standard price. At that time, Egyptian chariots delivered to Jerusalem could be purchased for 600 pieces of silver, and horses could be bought for 150 pieces of silver. Many of these were then resold to the kings of the Hittites and the kings of Aram. [2 Chronicles 1:13-17]

The way the Lord wants to bless you, silver and gold will be like the rocks in your driveway. Then it talks about all the other things: cedar wood, sycamore wood. All of this was so plentiful and it says when they began to purchase things the value went up. How would you like to buy a house for $100,000 and keep it for a year and it brings a half million? What if everything your hands touch prospers? Do you want to live in the good old days, or are you looking forward to the days ahead?

The Bible teaches that God's man asked for the right things and when he asked for the right things, everyone got blessed. My heart is for the nations of the world. I want to help other people. I still want to have a restaurants in other nations and hire people and let them make money and not have to depend on me – let God bless them.

I want to show you how you can keep the

THE LOVE OF MONEY

blessings of God in your life. Some of you say, "God I am sick and tired of being broke." What God did once, he can still do again. When you understand all this, whatever God promised 2,000 years ago is still working today.

God says, "Two thousand years ago I was wounded for your transgressions, bruised for iniquity, chastised and by my stripes you were healed. I saved you and I healed you." (Isaiah 53:5) Two thousand years later that is still working, folks. He is still saving and healing people. God said to Solomon, "If you ask for wisdom and knowledge of how to rule my people well, I will give you everything else in life."

I read this long before I became a preacher. I told God if He ever made me a pastor, I wanted to be like Solomon. Give me knowledge and wisdom, but God, if you call me to be a shepherd, the sheep should not die – the sheep should live. Any good shepherd takes care of his sheep and he makes sure the wolf doesn't come and kill his sheep.

There aren't any wolves where I live in Charlotte, but there are plenty of car wrecks. Now we have this new mosquito bite that kills you – West Nile. A lady here in North Carolina did die from it – a mosquito bite! I can tell you, when a mosquito bites me *it* is going to die. When he sucks blood out of this body, he is sucking Holy Ghost blood into his mouth. Just thump him off.

Some of you read these things and are full of fear. Some people are afraid if a mosquito bites a person with AIDS and then bites them, the disease will be transferred to them. The Bible says, *No weapon that is formed against you shall prosper.* [Isaiah 54:17] Whatever God spoke 2,000 or 6,000 years ago it should be working in right now. Jesus said, *Heaven and earth shall pass away but my words will never pass away.* [Matthew 24:35]

We need to come to the knowledge of the truth, to know that you have everything that pertains to life and godliness (2 Peter 1:3). You begin to say what the word says and people around you will complain that all you talk about is the Bible. Well, all the world talks about is killing, dying, and death. You can't even get out in the sun because it will kill you one day, so they say.

The Bible says, *When sin is finished, it brings forth death.* [James 1:15] It doesn't say a lot of hairspray will kill you. People say that hairspray is breaking down the ozone. No, I think it is sin breaking down the ozone. I believe sin is what is destroying the world. Isn't it unusual they changed the freon in America because it is going to break down the ozone and isn't it unusual that we pay through the nose for this new freon? We go right along with all this. "Yeah, it is all that hairspray we are using." I say it is the devil and the sin we are involved in that will kill us.

It is time we rise up and become the men and women God wants us to be. We have twisted the word of God around so much that we call bad good and good bad. I am trying to get you to say what the word says. Do you want to prosper and be in health even as your soul prospers?

When you come to the knowledge of the truth and you begin to say, "Lord, you have asked me, and I could ask for money but God I want to be a man or woman who knows how to take care of my family. Lord, I want to be a good mother or dad. I want to set examples for my children." God said, "I am going to give you everything everyone else wants because you asked me properly."

Deuteronomy 8:1 says, *Be careful to obey all the commandments I have given you today and then you will live and multiply and will live and occupy the land the Lord has sworn unto your ancestors.* What is the commandment of God in

THE TEMPTATIONS OF WEALTH

this day and age? It is to love God with all your heart and to love your neighbor as yourself. If I want God's blessings on my life, I have to love God and I have to love you.

The Bible says to love God and then love your neighbor as yourself. All these things will be added unto you – anything you want from God. The way you treat others is the way God is treating you. Solomon said, "Lord, give me the ability to rule and reign," and God said, "Fine – now I will give you everything else you need to do it."

Without wealth and riches, I don't care how much wisdom you have, you still have to pay a light bill, water bill, taxes, and insurance. God said that because you asked for it I will give you more than enough and you will have enough for everything else you want to do in this life. Be careful to keep all the commandments. *Remember how the Lord, your Father, led you through the wilderness for forty years, humbled you and tested you to improve your character and to feel out whether or not you would be ready to obey his commandments. Yes, he humbled you by letting you go through hunger and then feeding you through manna, a food previously unknown to you and your ancestors.* [Deuteronomy 8:2 NLT]

We need fresh manna. The Bible says, *Feeding you with manna, a food previously unknown to you and your ancestors. He did it to teach you that people need more than just bread for life – real life comes from feeding you every word of the Lord. For these forty years, your clothes didn't wear out and your feet did not blister or swell.* [vv. 3-4]

No member of my church has lost any babies. God has taken care my congregation since I began feeding them this word of faith, manna from heaven. Coming to my church isn't like going to a place and eating a hamburger or chicken – it is more than that. God told me, "I have raised this church to where it would give you the true bread of life." I have tried to teach you the ways of the Lord. I have tried to teach you that it isn't by working fifteen jobs a week. It isn't by working a hundred hours a week. That will never bring you to prosperity, folks. If that is true, then everyone in the world would be a millionaire. What makes you a millionaire is when you work somewhere, God blesses it, and you distribute the blessings of God, tithes, offerings, and gifts. I did that.

I blessed my people and gave to them. God said, "Someone ought to take you out to dinner.

Someone will fill your car up with gasoline. When your car tears up somebody will fix it for you free. When you need tires they will be given to you." Everywhere you turn, the blessings of God come in. They just shower on you. It says it all happens because you obey His commandments.

God is saying, "I have brought you to a point, children of Israel, where I can take care of you and bless you and it doesn't come from natural food – it comes from spiritual food – the word of God. Most of you have gone to church all your life and played the religious games. The service lasts from 11 to 12. You heard the two songs of doxology, the first and last stanzas of poems. You saw the *Look* magazine; you heard the preacher preach his 15-20 minute message – you were out the door and you were dying!

I found out the Bible says shepherds take care of the sheep. It doesn't say the sheep take care of the shepherd. When you take care of the sheep, God will take care of you.

The Bible says, *For all the forty years I clothed you they never wore out, and your feet did not blister or swell. So you should realize that just as a parent disciplines a child the Lord, your God disciplines you to help.* [Deuteronomy 8:4-5 NLT]

All that means is that God is going to take care of you. He will correct you. How many times have we looked and said, "Yeah, God is going to beat on 'em." Have you ever had a child that did something wrong and you set him down to talk to him and he understood? You didn't have to slap him in the face and kick his teeth out of his mouth. God said He will correct you and talk to you. How does God talk to us—with a hand or with a stick? He talks to us through His word; and he does it as a loving parent would do. The Bible says, *All Scripture is inspired by God and is useful to teach us what is true and to make us realize what is wrong in our lives. It straightens us out and teaches us to do what is right. It is God's way of preparing us in every way, fully equipped for every good thing God wants us to do.* [2 Timothy 3:16-17 NLT]

Through His living word, He woos you to a place of repentance. Do you understand what I am saying? Some of you think God is going to kill you. God said, "I love you. I have done all of this for you."

So, obey the commandments of the Lord God by walking in his ways and fearing him. The Lord your God is bringing you into a good land of flowing streams, pools of water with springs that gush forth in the valley and in the hill. It is a land of wheat, barley, grapes, figs and pomegranates, olives and honey. It is a land where food is plentiful and nothing is lacking. It is a land where iron is common, stone is common, copper is in abundance and when you have eaten your fill, praise the Lord your God for the good land he has given you. [Deuteronomy 8:6-10 NLT]

Most people pray over their food before they eat it. We pray before, but the Bible doesn't say that. It says, *After you have eaten and after you are full, then praise God for it.* [v. 10] We have it backwards. I go to restaurants and no one sees me praying and they all think the preacher doesn't pray. I wait until after I am through to thank God for it. We do things our own way instead of doing things the way God instructed. The Bible says to praise the Lord for the good land he has given you, but this is the time to be careful. When you have money, houses, land, and food – this is the time to be careful.

But that is the time to be careful! Beware that in your plenty you do not forget the Lord your God and disobey his commands, regulations, and laws. For when you have become full and prosperous and have built fine homes to live in and when your flocks and herds have become very large and your silver and gold have been multiplied along with everything else, that this is the time to be careful. Do not become proud at that time and forget your Lord your God who rescued you out of slavery in the land of Egypt. Do not forget that he led you through the great and terrifying wilderness with poisonous snakes and scorpions, where it was so hot and dry. He gave you water from the rock! He fed you with manna in the wilderness, a food unknown to your ancestors. He did this to humble you and test you for your own good. He did it so you would never think that it was your own strength and energy that made you wealthy. Always remember that it is the Lord your God who gives you power to become rich, and he does it to fulfill the covenant he made with your ancestors. [Deuteronomy 8:11-18 NLT]

This is important. Remember that God brought you here when you had nothing; and when you have plenty, don't act proud and arrogant. Remember what God did for you; and when you have more, you will give more! That is what

He is telling you here. Don't become proud and think that your own strength and energy made you wealthy. Always remember that is the Lord your God who gave you the power to become wealthy. He did this to fulfill His covenant that He made with our ancestors.

The passage ends with this: *But I assure you of this: If you ever forget the Lord your God and follow other gods, worshiping and bowing down to them, you will certainly be destroyed. Just as the Lord has destroyed other nations in your path, you also will be destroyed for not obeying the Lord your God.* [Deuteronomy 8:19-20 NLT]

If you ever forget the Lord your God, and follow after other things, it will cost you. God tells us in the very first part of this, "I want to bring you to places; I want to take you places; I want to bless you. But, when I do all this for you be very careful because at that moment it will be the greatest testing of your life – when you have abundance in your life. When you get there remember from where God brought you. In other words, you should remember when you get to this place, that you were in bondage and led a very poor life, but all of a sudden God brought you out and gave you plenty. At that moment "Beware – this will be the

THE LOVE OF MONEY

greatest test!"

Did you notice the Lord didn't say the greatest test would come in poverty? No, He said that the greatest test will be when you have plenty of money.

Most of us can't handle money. The more we get, the more we spend and we are under the pressures of life. You know how easy it is to say, "I have plenty. I don't have to try like I used to and I can ease up right now." God says, "No, remember I brought you up and you had nothing when you got here." I remember the first church service I went to I had $90 in my pocket and I put every dime in the offering plate. I have never been broke since. The testing isn't when you have the $90. The testing is when you have the $750,000 in real estate. The testing comes now when you can take the gold and hand it to somebody – not when somebody gave you the gold.

Then He says, *If you ever forget the Lord your God and follow other gods of worship or bow down to them, you will certainly be destroyed.* Money will destroy you if you don't handle it correctly in your life. Money will be your god. You will become ineffective. You will not go out and become a soul winner. You won't give to the missions because rather than give your money, you will hoard your money. It says, *Just as the Lord has destroyed all nations in your path, you will also be destroyed for not obeying your God.* [v. 20]

Chapter 9 of Deuteronomy begins like this: *Hear, O Israel! Today you are about to cross the Jordan River to occupy the land belonging to nations much greater and more powerful than you. They live in cities with walls that reach to the sky! They are strong and tall-descendants of the famous Anakite giants. You've heard the saying, 'Who can stand up to the Anakites?' But the Lord your God will cross over ahead of you like a devouring fire to destroy them. He will subdue them so that you will quickly conquer them and drive them out, just as the Lord has promised. After the Lord your God has done this for you, don't say to yourselves, 'The Lord has given us this land because we are so righteous!' No, it is because of the wickedness of the other nations that he is doing it. It is not at all because you are such righteous, upright people that you are about to occupy their land. The Lord your God will drive these nations out ahead of you only because of their wickedness, and to fulfill the oath he had sworn to your ancestors Abraham, Isaac, and Jacob. I will say it again: The Lord your God is not giving you this good land because you are righteous, for you are not—you are a stubborn people.* [Deuteronomy 9:1-6 NLT]

God said to me, "I am not going to bless Freedom Christian Center because of your righteousness, but I am going to do it because I have a covenant with my Son."

That's why I try to keep my relationship strong with Jesus. He was doing it because He made a promise and not because we are good. Apart from Jesus we are not one bit good. It was because He made a promise. I was reading this and God asked, "Do you know why I will take care of you? Because I made a covenant with My Son that I would take care of you." That's the reason for eternal security; that's the reason you have everlasting life with God.

God said, "Don't come to Me and think I am blessing you because of your own righteousness. I am blessing you because of what My Son did. It's His righteousness that gets you blessed and makes you righteous."

Thank God for His promises! By His stripes I am healed! Thank God that He took on all the bruises and iniquity that I could be free from sin. I am not earning it; I am getting it by grace. I am getting it because He just loves me because I believe what Jesus did was good enough for me. Then He tells me that everything I touch will prosper. It doesn't say because of me, but because of what He did. Jesus walked 3-1/2 years in absolute prosperity. He had no need of anything. He could feed everyone in town and have plenty left over.

Sometimes He would be limited to a couple of fish and a couple pieces of bread. But after feeding 5,000 men, they had twelve baskets left over. I want to live like that. I can do it as long as I am in Him. He is in me, and I am not in it for the money.

We have a relationship with the Father and He has promised us this: money will be no problem soon. The wealth of the sinners is laid up for the just. There are a few Christians who are not just and they will go in to poverty. If you put your money in stocks you will go bankrupt. A 401(K) is not guaranteed money. It is investment money and you are hoping it will double, quadruple, like any other. The Lord is greater than anything down here. If you serve God, His blessings will find you and overtake you (Deuteronomy 28:15).

God, we give our very best to You today. We give our lives and our finances. You have ordained raises, promotions, job opportunities, pensions, and dreams to Your people. Thank You that You have given them long life, health and prosperity. Father, we have heard the word of God; we have eaten fresh manna. We realize all the gold and silver is coming our way. We know that prosperity is Your will and we are now living in the Promised Land. In the midst of all those trials and temptations of prosperity, we will be faithful to You. We will not turn from You to worship something other than You. We will be continuously faithful. In Jesus' name.

CHAPTER FIVE

Put Your Money to Work

To those who use well what they are given, even more will be given, and they will have an abundance. But from those who are unfaithful, even what little they have will be taken away.
—Matthew 25:29 NLT

Every person has been given talents and abilities from God, but they rarely do anything with them. It's important to understand the God desires that you put what He gives you to work to benefit the kingdom. Jesus said, *Again, the kingdom of heaven can be illustrated by a story of a man going on a trip. He called together his servants and gave them money to invest for him while he was gone. He gave five bags of gold to one, two bags of gold to another, and one bag of gold to the last—dividing it in proportion to their own abilities—and left on his trip.* [Matthew 25:14-15 NLT]

I want you to understand what the Lord is saying about "dividing it in proportion to their abilities". As a pastor, there is more responsibility on me than it is on you. That's the reason God called me to be a pastor. He knew that I could take the responsibility. If you were up here trying to lead a church of 250 people, you may not be able to handle the pressure.

When the master left on the trip, *the servant who received the five bags of gold began immediately to invest the money and soon doubled it. The servant with two bags of gold also went right to work and doubled the money. But the servant who received one bag of gold dug a hole in the ground and hid the master's money for safekeeping.* [Matthew 25:16-18 NLT]

The one who had the single bag of gold illustrates what most people do with their abilities. They never do anything with them. How many people work a job right now? You know you are responsible for every dime you have made in your whole life? Think about it. If you made $20,000 a year for fifty years you would make $1,000,000! Most of us will work for fifty years and most of us will make at least $20,000 a year. At the end of your life God will ask, "What did you do with my $1,000,000?"

Most of you will say, "Lord, I put $100,000 in the church."

And God will answer, "What did you do with the $900,000?"

That's what we have to give an account for — not the $100,000. The question is "What did you do with the $900,000?"

Most people will say, "Lord, I paid the light bill, phone bill, taxes, insurance. Lord, I had nothing left over." Some people will say "Lord, I took that $900,000 and paid the light bill, phone bill, taxes, insurance and I invested it and bought homes, bonds, and savings accounts. Lord, when I died I still had $150,000 left over."

This is what the story is all about — what did you do with your money that God gave you? It doesn't say 'talents' in the New Living Translation. It gets right to the point and says, "What did you do with the money I put in your hands?" Look how these people responded back to him.

After a long time their master returned from his trip and called them to give an account on how they had used his money. The servants to whom he had entrusted with the five bags of gold said, 'Sir, you gave me five bags of gold to invest and I have doubled that amount.' The master was full of praise. 'Well done, my good and faithful servant. You have been faithful in handling this small amount. Now I will give you many more responsibilities. Let's celebrate together.' Next came the servant who had received the two bags of gold with the report, 'Sir, you gave me two bags of gold to invest and I have doubled that amount.' The master said, 'Well done, my good and faithful servant. You have been faithful in handling this small amount so now I will give you more responsibility. Let us celebrate together.' Then the servant with the one bag of gold said, 'Sir, I knew you are a hard man, harvesting crops you didn't plant and gathering crops you didn't cultivate. I was afraid I would lose your money so I hid it in the earth and here it is. But, the master replied, 'You wicked and lazy servant. You think I'm a hard man, do you harvesting crops I didn't plant and gathering crops I didn't cultivate? Well, you should at least have put my money into the bank so I could have some interest. Take the money from this servant and give it to the one with ten bags of gold. [Matthew 25:19-28]

That's the reason I am always challenging people. If you don't have money in the bank, somewhere along the line you will answer to God for that. A lot of time people say that when the

Lord comes back it will make no difference. It must make a difference because God tells you right here: "If you are not doubling what I put in your hand then at least put it somewhere and make me something out of it." Folks, I read this long before I became a pastor. You all think I am trying to find something to preach to you. If you would get a Bible and read it, you would realize that it's not wrong to save a dollar a week or five dollars a week or at least put it in a savings account. Just don't spend it!

Some of you might say, "Brother, what if we die and all that money is in the bank?" Then God is going to call you a good and faithful servant. At least you put it somewhere and made interest off it. He's going to ask, "Why didn't you at least put it in the bank and draw some interest off that $1,000,000 I gave you the last fifty years?

Most people spend the money on themselves – self-gratification. God has no problem with that but He asks, "Did you leave any of it for Me? Did you invest any of My money?"

That's the reason I am trying to get you to invest at least something. Find something to get involved in. If you can't give $100 a week, at least put a dollar a week into three nations of the world.

He is going to say, "Well done, My good and faithful servant." Do you understand what I am saying? I just put out the challenge. But God is going to look at it differently. Jesus said that the woman who put two mites in the treasury put in more than all the others because out of her love for God, she gave all she had (Mark 12:44).

Some of you may only have a small amount to invest and it was the best you can do. You may say that isn't much money, but God is saying, "No, they put more in than the ones that put hundreds or thousands in." God doesn't look at it the same way we do. He looks at the heart (1 Samuel 16:7).

This story is not about what you can do on this earth, but what you will do in the life to come. What are you most concerned about? What you have now or what you will have one day for God? Some people are storing up for today, but some of us are storing up for tomorrow. God doesn't look at the amount. He looks at what you are doing for His kingdom whether it be five bags of gold, two bags of gold or one bag of gold.

God was not angry because the servant hid the money. God was angry because he didn't do anything with his talents. It says right here, *You are a wicked man. Take the money from the servant and give it to the one that has ten bags of gold. To those who use well what they are given even more will be given to them. But from those who are unfaithful, even what little they have will be taken from them.* [Matthew 25:26-29 NLT]You should be shouting right now.

There isn't any way in the world you can stay on a $20,000 a year salary if you are hearing what I am saying to you. God says that the ones who have the most will be the ones who do well with what is given them; and "I will give them more than what they have."

I don't care if you make $40,000 or $20,000 a year, you will never have enough. People tickle me – they wad that dollar bill up like they are ashamed of it. Spread it out! Some of you should just stop and say, "God, thank You that You have given me the ability to give. Thank You, Lord. This is not a million dollars, but I thank You. Everything I give is given back to me." Give rejoicing because you have ministered to the Lord.

Respect God. What I have isn't mine – it belongs to God. If you read these stories it will let you know. *To the unfaithful one, even what little they have will be taken away. Now throw this useless servant into outer darkness where there is wailing and gnashing of teeth.* [vv.29-30]

Literally, Jesus is not talking about going to hell here. He is not dealing with heaven and hell. Let me tell you, folks, have you ever felt like your whole life was just a mess? Do you sometimes say to yourself, "I never have enough" and every week it seems like you are one week behind on your bills. He is dealing with you being blessed or cursed. Is your life a blessing or a curse?

You are determining your own destiny right now. In the next passage the Lord talks about heaven or hell and the separation of the righteous from the unrighteous. It says *But, when the Son of man comes in his glory and all his angels with him, then he sits upon the glory of his throne, then all the nations will be gathered in his presence and he will separate the sheep from the goats. He will place the sheep on his right hand and the goat on the left hand. Then the king will say to those on his right hand, come – you are blessed of my Father – inherit the kingdom prepared for you from the foundation form. When I was hungry you fed me. When I was thirsty, you gave me drink. I was a stranger and you invited me into your home. I was naked and you gave me clothes. I was sick and you cared for me. I was in prison and you visited me.*

These righteous ones would reply, 'Lord, when did we see you hungry and fed you or thirsty and gave you something to drink, or a stranger and we let you in, when were you naked and we gave you clothes, when were you in prison and we visited you?' The king then told them, 'When you did it unto one of the least of my brothers and my sisters, you were doing it unto me.' Then the king will turn to those on his left hand and say, 'Away with you, you cursed ones into the eternal fire prepared for the devil and his demons!' [Matthew 25:31-41 NLT]

I don't want to be one of the cursed ones. Do you see this? You all are thinking in the sweet by and by and I am thinking about the nasty now and now. I feel like I have already been separated. I am a sheep or a goat right now, folks. I am either righteous or unrighteous. I am either blessing the work of God or I am stealing from Him.

Jesus continues, *When I was hungry you didn't feed me. When I was thirsty you didn't give me drink. I was a stranger and you didn't invite me into your home. I was naked and you didn't give me any clothes. I was sick and in prison and you didn't visit me. Then they said, 'Lord, when were you hungry or thirsty, naked or sick, or in prison and we didn't help you?' I will reply, 'When you refuse to help the least of my brothers and sisters, you have refused to help me.' They will go away into eternal punishment and the righteous will go into eternal life.* [vv.42-46]

As I said before, you are determining your destiny right now. Where do you want to spend eternity? Are you prepared for His coming? No one will know the hour or the minute, but the Bible says you will know the seasons and the times of the coming of God (Acts 1:7). He said when He comes back He will find a church without spot or blemish.

He said it like this, "I will find a church full of My power that is looking for My appearance" (Hebrews 9:28). If you are not looking for an appearance, folks, you will not see it. You will miss that day! I want to be alive for that day.

God is warning us. "How are you treating the things I left behind right now?" If you won a $1,000,000, would that change your whole perception of life? How would you treat it? God knows how you would treat it. You'd say, "Oh, if I won it I would put my tithes in." You know what? If God gave you $1,000,000 you wouldn't put the tithes in, because if you don't tithe on the $20,000 you make now, what makes you think you would tithe on a million?

I didn't write the word of God, folks. God did. I love money, but why do I love money? Do I love it in order to heap upon my own lust, or to do something for God? You have to make those decisions by reading the word of God and determining that you are going to follow the destiny of the word of God.

I am trying to tell you to get ready for what God is about to do. In Luke 19:11-27 we read that *the crowd was listening to everything Jesus said. Because he was near Jerusalem, he told the story to correct the impression that the Kingdom of God would begin right away.*

'A nobleman was called away to a distant empire to crown a king, and then return. Before he left he gathered together ten servants. He gave them ten pounds of silver to invest while he was gone, but his people hated him and sent a delegate after him to say they did not want him to be their king.' Then he returned and the king called into service those to whom he had given the money. He wanted to find out what they had done with the money and what their profits were.

The first servant reported him a tremendous gain. Ten times as much as he was originally given. 'Well done,' the king proclaimed. 'You are a trustworthy servant. You have been faithful with the little I have entrusted you, so you will be governor of ten cities as your reward.'

Look at that, folks. God said, "Because you were faithful I will give you ten cities as your reward.' The next servant made five times the original amount. 'Well done,' the king said. 'You can be governor over five cities.'"

Are you understanding this? God said, "I will give you cities to rule over." Some of you will rule over ten cities and some will rule over five.

"The third servant brought back only the original amount of money and said, 'I hid it and kept it safe.' I was afraid because you are a hard man to deal with, taking what isn't yours and harvesting crops you didn't plant.'"

I want you to notice that one servant earned ten times more, one servant earned five times more, and one servant hid it. What about the other seven servants? Where are they? He gave them all ten bags of gold, but what happened to the other seven?

Jesus said that there was a delegation of servants that said, "We don't want you to be over us." It was like they were saying, "We appreciate what you have given us but you aren't going to tell us what to do with it." Years ago, I read this, and it gave me great respect for God – how I treat God's money and how I treat God's possessions in my life. God, tell me what to do with what you give me. I want to take care of what you put into my hand every day, Lord, because I am responsible for it.

'You wicked servant!' the king roared. 'Hard, am I? If you knew so much about me and how tough I am, why didn't you deposit the money in the bank so I could at least get some interest on it?'

If you think God is so mean, you had better do something with His money then. I know you all don't talk like this, but you meet people every day that make stupid statements about the God that you serve.

Are you listening to me? I remember being a policeman – I wasn't even serving God – and this man ran off the road and hit two or three cars and rammed into a building and when we got there he was dead. I knew he didn't die in the car wreck so we had to take him out of the car and they did an autopsy on him and found out he had a heart attack. The insurance company called me and asked my opinion whether the man had a heart attack before running into the building, or did he hit the building and then have a heart attack. I said, "What's the difference?"

I figured he had a heart attack and died and then ran into cars and hit the building. The insurance adjuster said, "If he had a heart attack, had a wreck and then hit the building, then we can call it an 'act of God'. But if he had the heart attack after the wreck, they would have to pay the claim." What he was saying was that if God had killed him, they wouldn't have to pay the claim.

So I said, "That's the way it happened. He had the heart attack after the wreck." Just like that it came out of my mouth. I wasn't even serving God, but I wasn't about to say that God killed that man, causing him to hit two or three cars and run into a building. I had such a fear inside of me that I said he died after he did all that stuff. He asked how I knew that and I told him that was my opinion as a police officer, and that's what he had asked me for. They had to pay all those claims.

The Lord says right here, *If you thought I was that mean, that hard and that cruel, why didn't you at least invest some of my money in the bank so I could get some interest back? Then turning to the others standing by, the king ordered, 'Take the money from this servant and give it to the one that earned the most. But, Master, the servant has already enough. 'Yes,' the king replied, 'but those who use it well even more will be given to them, but to those who are unfaithful even what little they have will be taken away. And now about these enemies of mine who didn't want me to be their king – bring them in and execute them right in my presence.* [Luke 19:22-27 NLT]

Deal with them! That's the reason you need to deal with all your problems, folks, because if you don't deal with them one day God will deal with them. Remember, this Bible is not written to the ungodly – it is written to servants of God. He is asking you servants of God – how do you treat what I give you?

I love money – I love it. The reason I love it is that I want to do more for God. I want to know whether God will take care of us or whether He won't take care of us. If you take what God has given you and do something with it, He will give you more. God doesn't want you to make $25,000 for the next twenty years. He wants to bless you.

Going from $25,000 to $28,000 is not a blessing. It's called a "cost of living raise."

Have you noticed gasoline is going up like crazy again? How would you like to have enough money where that doesn't bother you? I am telling you right now, God wants to do something. I have proven to you that we can pay off our debts and still be blessed by God. We can still do missionary work and still be blessed by God.

As I wrote before, I don't care what the stock market is doing. I didn't come this far to get into some kind of financial crunch that is coming on the world right now. I don't care what goes on around me. God is still the Source in my life.

All the wells are not dry yet. All the water has not run out of the river yet. Years ago we had a deficit of twenty inches of rain in North Carolina. You know what that means right now to the system of water? There is a depreciation of blessings right there. Things are drying up and I am watching it. I am telling you God says that if we get ready, it won't touch us.

God spoke to Joseph and said, "There are going to be seven years of famine but I am going to take care of you in the midst of the famine" (Genesis 41:25-32). I am telling you that God will take care of us in the midst of famine. We are not going to stop the projects of what we are doing. I don't care how scarce things get. Are you listening to me? I am telling you God is getting ready to bless you. We are blessed coming in and blessed going out. Your whole life will change for the next twenty years. You won't have to worry about whether there is a lay-off – you won't care. God said, "I will bless you all." I believe the blessings are out there.

CHAPTER SIX

God, Reveal Yourself to Me

Who has believed our report and who is the arm of God going to be revealed to? —Isaiah 53:1 [NLT]

I am calling you to renew your covenant. Not with God but with each other. God desires to see you succeed and be promoted. In this season and time, the Lord is calling you to restore your covenant vows one with another. "Then, the rains will come on this dry land. They will fall and break up fallow ground and righteousness will be restored in the midst of My people," says God. "I am calling you back to your knees. I am calling you back to your face. You have lost your desire to seek Me and for that reason your land is sick and your land is weary and your land is dying. But, My word says that 'if My people would humble themselves and pray and seek My face, then I will hear from heaven and I will heal your land.' Renew your covenant one with another, for you have called right wrong and wrong right and this day I am calling you back to your knees. The people that love me, that are chosen for the priesthood, they are chosen and set apart for me. I have called you out of darkness into the marvelous light and you have returned to darkness. Have you returned to the pit? My right hand is ever long to pull you out. I have set your feet on solid rock. I have took out your heart of stone and traded it with a heart of flesh. I inscribed your name in the palm of My hand and no man will pluck you out of My hand," says God. "Renew your vows with Me and others," says God, "and the rain will fall once again on this dry land."

God is reminding us about falling in love with each other and if we are in love with each other, then all of a sudden God said, "I will bless you – I will take care of you all."

I remember when I was first called into the ministry of an apostle. I didn't want to talk about it because I didn't want people to address me as Apostle. Then God spoke to me and He said, "The calling of an apostle is not something you earn; it is something that I give you." It is a gift. I didn't choose to be an apostle. I chose to be a Christian – just be happy to go to Heaven. In the midst of that I made myself available to the ministry. Many of you all would love to be involved in the ministry. God showed me years ago that to be involved in the ministry, you have to turn the pendulum to 51% of your life to the things of God and 49% to the things of the world.

However, most of us work 40-50 hours a week. We have commitments to our job, our home, and then somewhere in the middle, we take five or even twenty minutes and read the Bible. Or maybe you have a daily devotion and you read it and you realize you only give 1% of your life to God. Then you get frustrated because you would like to do more for God, but you have to get that pendulum to swing.

God began to speak to me years ago about giving 90% of my income away. I didn't go from 10% to 90%. I couldn't do that because I owed everybody. When you owe bills and you are in bondage to finances, you can't give it. I started making commitments to God, for Him to help me get out of debt. I haven't made a car payment since 1967. I bought a 1972 Pontiac Grand Prix for my wife and paid cash for it. I haven't made a house payment since 1968.

I made commitments to God to help me to get

out from under the world's pressures. Think about this. I was watching television the other night and they were talking with some financial advisors. There was a man who owed thousands of dollars on credit cards and he made a statement that if he made the minimum payments, it would take him over twelve years to pay it off. A lot of you have three or four credit cards that are charging you 18-21% interest. If you have three credit cards that are charging you 21%, that's 60% interest you are paying, which means if you owe $5,000 you are paying $3,000 a year just in interest. If you multiply that times the minimum payments, you will never get out of debt.

I am challenging you to think. I think if you would start thinking with your heart, God can get you out of debt and turn things around. God is reminding us to fall in love with each other and then God says, "I am going to bless you and take care of you all."

Isaiah 53 begins, *Who has believed our report and who is the arm of God going to be revealed to?* This explains something – who is going to believe the things of God and to whom God is going to reveal himself. Most people have little or no knowledge of God. The only thing they know about God is that God destroyed the earth by water. He destroyed Sodom and Gomorra and all they think about is death. They really don't know God. They don't know how much God loves them. God reveals His love through the gospels—through Jesus. God Himself came to this earth and purchased us back and gave us back the authority, the keys to the kingdom, and said, "The earth is yours again." Now in two thousand years look at the mess we have made.

Quoting the prophet Isaiah, I say, "Who is going to believe this report; and who will allow God's arm to be revealed?" Who is going to allow God to reveal Himself to them now? How many of you believe that God will communicate to your needs and take care of your life and watch over you so that no weapon formed against you will prosper?

God is in your life. A woman made a statement the other day about her husband who had died. She said that he had "to go be with God." I walked out of that building and I thought, "God, I don't want to die to be with You. I am already with You. You are living in me. You took Your abode in me." The Bible says, *Greater is he that is in me than he that is in the world.* [1 John 4:4]

I am full of the greater One today. Jesus said, "If I go away, I will duplicate Myself in the Holy Ghost" – He will come and live inside of you. God is saying, "Who can I reveal Myself to? Who will believe My report?"

Then Isaiah starts talking about Jesus, that when He grew up they didn't see Him as who He really was. He grew up as a carpenter's boy and then all of a sudden it switches over to the cross and it begins to talk about how He was marred and beaten and nobody wanted to look at Him. We put a cross on the wall and have Jesus nailed to it but we cover His private organs. This is not correct because Jesus was literally a naked man when He hung on that cross. That was the reason His mother stood far off and wouldn't look upon His nakedness. She didn't want to bring shame to Him. Literally, they stripped Jesus until He was naked. Can you imagine the Son of God being hung from a cross in a naked position where every man and every woman could look on His nakedness and His family honored Him by standing afar off.

For he shall grow up before him as a tender plant, and as a root out of a dry ground. He had no form nor comeliness; and when we shall see him, there is no beauty that we should desire him. He is despised and rejected of men; a man of sorrows, and acquainted with grief; and we hid as it were our faces from him. He was despised and we esteemed him not. Surely he has borne our griefs, and carried our sorrows. Yet we did esteem him stricken, smitten of God and afflicted. But he was wounded for our transgressions; he was bruised for our iniquities; the chastisement of our peace was upon him; and with his stripes we are healed. [Isaiah 53:2-5]

Literally, Jesus was a man of sickness and disease for us when He was on the cross. In addition to bearing all the sins of the world, Jesus also bore all of our sicknesses and diseases (Matthew 8:16-17). We are not *going* to get healed by his stripes – we *are* all healed (1 Peter 2:24). God's word says that we can get ourselves right spiritually and physically so that we don't have to live our lives in sickness and disease and poverty and, even in death. We have a right because Jesus paid for it. Thank God I am not *going to Heaven*, I am *already living in Heaven*. I am not going to get saved – I am already born again and I have eternal life.

Whose report are you going to believe? Who

is going to allow God's arm to be revealed to them? Who is going to believe that they have a new nature in their life, cleansed by the blood of Jesus, set apart for the work of God, healed by the power of God, delivered from the hands of Satan? Who is going to believe it?

God tells you, "I was wounded, and bruised – I took everything so that you can be free today." No wonder the devil doesn't want the body of Christ to expand. No wonder he wants death and destruction and addiction, and homosexuality to rule. He doesn't want us to get free because the minute we get free, we will be free, indeed.

I don't know about you, but I am free today! I can go eat and go drink without condemnation and guilt today. I know Jesus paid the price. I didn't do it by my good works or my works of righteousness, or how many times I went to church, or how many dollars I put in the offering plate. God did it for me when I was no good; when I was on my way to hell; when I didn't even have eternal life. My name was written in the Lamb's book of life because He saw in eternity that I would accept that sacrifice.

God said, "I wrote your name in there before the foundation of the world. Before you were born, you were in My life." Do you understand what this means? God said, "I did all this for you." He wants to give everyone of us the same opportunity as the ones before us. What God did for Paul and Peter, He wants to do in our lives.

You will determine your own destiny by the way you respond to God – the way you feel about Him today – what He means to you today. How do you think about God today? How big is your God today? Do you believe His report? Is He first place in your life?

It makes the devil mad when you talk like that. Monday morning you go to work and your boss says, "I don't understand it, but we are doubling your paycheck." You go to work tomorrow and you will get a promotion. God is saying, "Who can I reveal Myself to today?" God has His hand open to you. He wants to show you that He is a God of abundance today. He isn't a God of death and destruction. Call Him el Shadi – the breasted one, the healed one – the only one. Thank God I am healed today.

How will you see God today? Are you going to see Him as a serpent on the cross or will you see Him as your King and Lord? Will you see Him as a wounded and broken man, or do you see Him as a healed man sitting on a throne waiting for you to put all of His enemies under His feet. Is God everything you want? Is He everything you desire and thirst for? Is there yet another well for you to drink from? Is there still another cup you are looking for? Or, have you found the real cup – the real water? Have you found the real manna of life? Have you discovered and found who God really is? Is He everything that you need today? Will you allow Him to come into the secret chambers of your life today to fill up every avenue and crack of your life? God will not force His way into any man's life. Will you allow God to reveal Himself to you as to who He really is? You must see His report before you see His arm. The Bible says, *When thou shall make his soul an offering for sin, he shall see his seed, he shall prolong his days, and the pleasure of the LORD shall prosper in his hands.* [Isaiah 53:10]

I believe there was a place where the devil couldn't touch Job. This place was in Christ and we have this right now. God said, "Enough is enough." Romans 5:6 says, *For when we were yet without strength, in due time Christ died for the ungodly.* It was time and God said, "I am ready to restore, give back, pour back, give more – I will double – I will bring increase – I am ready to do it for you, Job. I will give you everything you lost. I am handing it back to you even this day."

Through Jesus, God has ordained increase, opened windows, pressed down and shaken together. He has brought deliverance, and everything a man needs for life and godliness on this earth (2 Peter 1:3).

God told Jesus that He would prolong His days. Jesus said, "Make My soul an offering for sin today. Come on, allow Me – permit Me – give Me the opportunity to prolong the days. Let Me have pleasure in the prosperity of My brethren." You have to allow Him to come into your natural and spiritual heart today. You must allow the Creator of the universe to be your Lord. You must. You have to. He will never finish what He starts in you unless you allow Him.

God, reveal yourself! God did it in the upper room. When Jesus began to break bread with the disciples, He saw strife and division. Right in the midst of that, God still had receptacles–people who wanted it. God may have had denial and strife and all that stuff, but in the midst of that, there was good, rich fertile soil.

It wasn't all waste ground; it wasn't all thorns

and thistles. There was a group in that upper room who were hungry; they were thirsty. They wanted the Lord to wash their feet – they wanted a part of His kingdom.

Isaiah continues, *He shall see the travail of his soul and shall be satisfied. By his knowledge shall my righteous servant justify many; for he shall bear their iniquities. Therefore, I will divide him a portion with the great and he shall divide the spoil with the strong. Because he has poured out his soul unto death; and he was numbered with the transgressors, and he bore the sin of many; and made intercession for the transgressors.* [Isaiah 53:11-12]

God promised this earth to the men and women here today. The Lord said He would never take it away. God promised He would not allow a flood to come on this earth to destroy mankind again. He is not in the destruction business. He is in the restoration business. Tribulation in this world is not God's plan. It is the resistance of mankind against the things of God. God wants His will to be done on earth as it is in heaven (Matthew 6:10). He desires to prove His will and purpose for mankind, but we have to renew our minds to the truth of God's word (Romans 12:2).

THE LOVE OF MONEY

We can taste of that fruit right now. Why do you have to wait until tomorrow to eat an apple when you have the fruit today in your mouth? Why do you have to wait until tomorrow to break bread when you can eat now? Why do you have to wait another day to drink of the wine? You can drink of the juice and enjoy your salvation in this life. You can enjoy your healing in this life. You can enjoy all the promises of God. God said, "The wealth of the sinner is laid up for the just."

Whose report will you believe? Will you believe the newspaper that says homosexuality and profanity and perversion is running rampant? Or do you believe God's report that says that you are raising up a righteous people – a holy people – literally, the elect. You must refuse to go under. Refuse to compromise the word. I refuse.

It is written in the book of Exodus that the children of Israel ate their Passover meal in a hurry. They didn't even wait until the next morning. They girded themselves – they prepared themselves. The LORD told them, *And thus shall you eat it, with your loins girded, your shoes on your feet, and your staff in your hand; and you shall eat it in haste. It is the LORD's passover.* [Exodus 12:11]

The next morning they all left with all the gold and silver and for forty years in the wilderness no one was weak. Right in the midst of a rebellion, God still blessed them. There's still a little rebellion left in me, but I deal with my rebellion. I want it to be just me and God living in this body. Let there be room enough only for God and what I am.

Are you all understanding this? Isaiah 54 begins like this: *"Sing, O childless woman! Break forth into loud and joyful song, O Jerusalem, even though you never gave birth to a child. For the woman who could bear no children now has more than all the other women," says the Lord. "Enlarge your house; build an addition; spread out your home!*

For you will soon be bursting at the seams. Your descendants will take over other nations and live in their cities. "Fear not; you will no longer live in shame. The shame of your youth and the sorrows of widowhood will be remembered no more, for your Creator will be your husband. The Lord Almighty is his name! He is your Redeemer, the Holy One of Israel, the God of all the earth. For the Lord has called you back from your grief-as though you were a young wife abandoned by her husband," says your God. "For a brief moment I abandoned you, but with great compassion I will take you back. In a moment of anger I turned my face away for a little while. But with everlasting love I will have compassion on you," says the Lord, your Redeemer. "Just as I swore in the time of Noah that I would never again let a flood cover the earth and destroy its life, so now I swear that I will never again pour out my anger on you." [Isaiah 54:1-9 NLT]

Those three bedroom houses aren't going to be big enough much longer. God said, "Believe My report and allow Me to reveal Myself to you." God is saying that there was a time you were childish – you didn't have anything. "Sing O childless woman! Break forth into loud and joyful song... for the woman who has no children has more than all the other women. Enlarge your house – build an addition to it. Spread out your home for you will soon be bursting at the seams."

I hope a few of you ladies go to the doctor and are told you have twins inside you. You will tell your husband, "Honey, this house will not hold all these kids – we will have to get a bigger house."

God said, "If you believe My report, and I will reveal Myself to you..." You have been barren long enough – you are ready to have children and when you start having children you had better build a bigger house because it won't hold them all. He said you had better put an addition onto it. You had better do something soon. The Bible says, "Your descendants will take over all nations and they will live in the city. Fear not, for you will no longer live in shame. The shame of your youth and the sorrow of your womanhood will be remembered no more. Your Creator will become your husband – your provider." He is going to watch out for us.

There is a place when God says, "Enough is enough." God said, "I want to do it now if you will allow Me to do it. I can be your Redeemer right now. I can be the Holy One of Israel right now – I can be your husband right now."

My God, don't wait another week for it. Start getting your dream house built – put the addition on your home. Let God see your house full of spiritual children if you don't want physical children.

God says, "It is time. I am the Lord God of Israel. I am your Redeemer. Will you allow Me today to reveal Myself to you? Just as I have sworn I will never destroy the earth again – you will never see My anger anymore. The mountains may depart and the hills disappear but even then I will remain loyal to you. No matter what you go through I will never leave you nor will I forsake you anymore."

We need to be become covenant people. I heard the story about a man of God who met this old Indian one day and said the old Indian wanted to blow on him. The Indian said it was customary that they go nose to nose and face to face. He said, "I am going to blow on you; everything I ever had is now yours." The man of God said that he blew back and he said, "I want you to have everything I have too."

Jesus walked in that upper room and the Bible says that He breathed on the disciples (John 20:22). In essence, He said, "Everything I have is now yours. I am in covenant with you today."

His blessings will never be broken. I believe this is ready to happen. I am not going by what I feel, taste, and touch. I am going by the word of God. I am telling you there is a God ready to bless. There is a God ready to touch. God said, "I am the God of this earth." "I am your Father and everything you want to be today." Thank you, Lord Jesus.

I want you to be excited. I want you to be covenant people. Instead of helping, you are trying to get ahead. Instead of trying to be equal, you are trying to step on others. We have to take care of someone other than ourselves. We have to love someone else rather than loving ourselves.

I remember as a kid we would become blood brothers with someone else. I wasn't even a Christian. I didn't understand. I was just a little boy, but there was something inside of me that I wanted to be a covenant brother with somebody else. Thank God we don't have to give up our blood. All we have to do is drink His blood. We don't have to give up our body. All we have to do is eat His body (John 6:53-54).

When you eat the bread and drink the blood of Jesus, you are a partaker of God's life. Let it come into your body and infiltrate every fiber of your being. I believe that is what God is saying. If we believe His report and will allow His arm to be revealed. If we will drink the blood and eat the bread, then He will show us what He has really done in our lives – how He saved us. We will see how He has healed and prospered us and how He has prolonged the days to give more people an opportunity to know Him.

THE LOVE OF MONEY

God gave me dreams and visions of this. It was not just a vision I had, but it was the heartbeat of the Father. I took that seed and showed them that the seed is not more important than the apple. It took the seed to produce the apple, but the apple is what is good to eat; and the seed has no value for me to eat. Only the fruit brings life to me. We want to become the trees and fruit of God. We want to become that which is edible – that which is good to this lost, dying world that is crying out for Him.

We don't want to be the seed – we want to be the fruit. The Lord Jesus is already the Seed, so we want to be the produce of fruit. God is the One that produces who you really are.

All our sins have been blotted out. We have a nature change. We have a new life today. We are not like we used to be. We live a repentant life, a blood-washed and sanctified life. We want to live a life that is pleasing to God.

CHAPTER SEVEN

God Is Shaking Things

For this is what the Lord Almighty says: In just a little while I will again shake the heavens and the earth. I will shake the oceans and the dry land, too. I will shake all the nations, and the treasures of all the nations will come to this Temple. I will fill this place with glory, says the Lord Almighty. —Haggai 2:6-7 NLT

I am excited about what God is doing. God wants to shake some things for us in order to bring the promises He made to pass. He wants to shake and stir up our remembrance to what He has done in the past, and what He desires to give us now. We see this in the book of Haggai when the Lord sent the prophet to deliver a message to the people.

"On August 29 of the second year of King Darius's reign, the Lord gave a message through the prophet Haggai to Zerubbabel son of Shealtiel, governor of Judah, and to Jeshua son of Jehozadak, the high priest. "This is what the Lord Almighty says: The people are saying, `The time has not yet come to rebuild the Lord's house- the Temple.' So the Lord sent this message

through the prophet Haggai: "Why are you living in luxurious houses while my house lies in ruins? This is what the Lord almighty God says, "Consider how things are going for you. You have planted much but harvested little. You have food to eat, but not enough to fill you up. You have wine to drink, but not enough to satisfy your thirst. You have clothing to wear, but not enough to keep you warm. Your wages disappear as though you were putting them in pockets filled with holes!

"This is what the Lord Almighty says: Consider how things are going for you!

Now go up into the hills, bring down timber, and rebuild my house. Then I will take pleasure in it and be honored, says the Lord. You hoped for rich harvests, but they were poor. And when you brought your harvest home, I blew it away. Why? Because my house lies in ruins, says the Lord Almighty, while you are all busy building your own fine houses. That is why the heavens have withheld the dew and the earth has withheld its crops. I have called for a drought on your fields and hills-a drought to wither the grain and grapes and olives and all your other crops, a drought to starve both you and your cattle and to ruin everything you have worked so hard to get." [Haggai 1:1-11 NLT]

Is this not self-explanatory? If you are having problems, check yourself out. If things aren't working out, find out what your priorities are. If your priorities are not in line with God and God's house and God's movement, then He is telling you that you will have problems.

In October 2001, we made a commitment to get our church out of debt – and we did it! Soon after, I had a pastor call me and he said, "I am going to be out of debt in less than two years. What you have done, I am going to do it too."

Another pastor called said, "I am telling you – I am getting out of debt. Starting in January we are paying our property off."

Are you listening to me, folks? Somehow they caught the vision that they don't have to be in debt anymore. The Bible says that the reason is because they are putting the things of God in first place. When they do that, God said that there will be plenty of rain, plenty of crops, plenty of oil. That means raises, employment, job opportunities, and inventions and dreams that will come to pass.

They obeyed the message from the Lord their God that had been delivered by the prophet

Haggai whom the Lord had sent and the people worshiped the Lord in earnest. Then Haggai and the messenger gave the people the message from the Lord. "I am with you, says the Lord!" [Haggai 1:12-13 NLT]

The minute the people got excited and were behind the message of the pastor and said, "We are going to do it – we are going to be out of debt if there isn't even a penny, we are going to do it." All of a sudden Haggai said, "I am with you, saith the Lord God."

"So the Lord sparked the enthusiasm of Zuburu, Joshua, the high priest and the whole realm of God's people and they began their work on the house of the God almighty. This was on September 21 of the second year of King Darius's reign. [Haggai 1:14-15 NLT]

Then on October 17 of that same year, the Lord sent another message through the prophet Haggai. "Say this to Zerubbabel son of Shealtiel, governor of Judah, and to Jeshua son of Jehozadak, the high priest, and to the remnant of God's people there in the land: Is there anyone who can remember this house-the Temple-as it was before? In comparison, how does it look to you now? It must seem like nothing at all! But now take courage, Zerubbabel, says the Lord. Take courage, Jeshua son of Jehozadak, the high priest. Take courage, all you people still left in the land, says the Lord. Take courage and work, for I am with you, says the Lord Almighty. My Spirit remains among you, just as I promised when you came out of Egypt. So do not be afraid. "For this is what the Lord Almighty says: In just a little while I will again shake the heavens and the earth. I will shake the oceans and the dry land, too. I will shake all the nations, and the treasures of all the nations will come to this Temple. I will fill this place with glory, says the Lord Almighty. The silver is mine, and the gold is mine, says the Lord Almighty. The future glory of this Temple will be greater than its past glory, says the Lord Almighty. And in this place I will bring peace. I, the Lord Almighty, have spoken!" [Haggai 2:1-9 NLT]

Some of you don't understand that. Remember how you felt when you first got saved? God is trying to say, "I know what you have been through. I have been with you the entire time, but I have to stir up your memory. Remember how you felt that day you came to God and said, "God, forgive me of my sins?" You wanted to tell everybody, "I am whole, I am clean, I am saved." Everybody looked at you like you were a nut because just two hours before that you were a no good sorry rascal. All of a sudden you are telling everyone that you are no longer a sinner. God says, "Remember that I am with you now just like when I brought you up out of sin. I am never going to leave you – I am never going to forsake you."

When the economy is sagging and things look tough – right in the middle of all this—don't be afraid. This is what the almighty God said, "In just a little while I will again shake the heavens and the earth." You think about it. We have a pecan tree on our property and there are so many pecans on that tree! If you had a big enough grip on that big tree and started shaking it, you would have enough pecans out there to fill up a pick-up truck.

We think that when God says, "He's going to shake things," that it means that God is out to get us. God won't get us. He is talking about how He is getting ready to bless everyone. This isn't doom and gloom that I hear shaking. Let me tell you, I got shook when I got saved. In 1958 He took me and shook me to the roots of my life. Surely I did not live up to all the potential of it. But you know the older I get, the more I want to live up to my potential. He said, "In just a little while I will shake the heavens and the earth and the oceans and the dry land too. I will shake all the nations and all the nations will come into My temple."

God said "I will shake it all loose." Folks, the temple is me and you. You are the church. You are the tabernacle of God. You are the city of Zion. Out of you will come forth the praises of God. He said, "I will shake the heavens and the earth."

You shouldn't be fearful of the enemy either. The Bible tells us not to be fearful, but to stand and resist the devil (Ephesians 6:11, James 4:7). Too many Christians aren't stepping out in faith for fear of being attacked by the devil. There are devils out there waiting on you, but you are protected, provided you keep on the armor God has given you. Fear strips you of this armor and gives the enemy access to you. Job said, *For the thing which I greatly feared is come upon me, and that which I was afraid of is come unto me.* [Job 3:25]

Remember those words. If a little demon will scare you, there are many more waiting to get you one day. Demons aren't your problem – you have authority over them. Similar to people who are afraid of swimming in the ocean for fear of sharks, people are afraid to get involved with what God is doing. Jesus called His disciples to "launch out into the deep water in order to get a haul of fish (Luke 5:4). Stay out of the water if you want to, but don't cry and complain that you are afraid of everything that comes along. God said, "I will shake the oceans and the dry land and the treasures of the nations will come to My people." You all should be shouting right now. Some of you are so broke you can't shout anymore.

He said, "The silver is Mine and the gold is Mine, says the Lord." He said, "The future glory of this temple will be greater than the past said the Almighty and in this place I will bring peace."

Some of you are asking, "How is He going to make me have peace?" Having your pockets full of money right now would make you happy, wouldn't it? I bet some of you could dance with the best of them if that were to happen. If someone knocks on your door and hands you a million dollar check, I promise you some of you will dance around the church – get down low, get up high – you won't care. What the Lord means by "glory" is that when God blesses you with silver and gold, then people will see that glory. When you go pay your house off tomorrow, you will have to tell them how God blessed you. They will see the glory of God when you hand them that $112,000 check and say, "I am out of debt."

Then they will do what the bank said to me, "Pastor Melton, if your church needs anymore money just call us."

I said, "We may call, but I believe there will be the day when we won't need you anymore – we will pay cash."

That was revealing the glory of God to that man. Most churches beat banks out of money, cheat them out of money. We never made a payment late – we paid our monthly payments in advance. You don't think they would call us today to see if we need anything from that bank? If I had been late, they wouldn't have called me. They would have called me and said, "foreclosure."

Folks, when He fills you up with blessings, you are filled with the glory of God. How do I know that? The Lord's word says, "The silver is Mine – the gold is Mine and the future glory of the temple is going to be greater than that which was in the past." Read about how God blessed the old folks and He said, "That's nothing to what I am going to do for your new folks."

THE LOVE OF MONEY

I am getting ready for my boat. Your boat sunk and sharks are moving around it and you are afraid to dive for it. He said, "In this place I bring peace." Folks, how will you have peace? When you are out of debt, you will feel like a different person. When you owe no man anything but the love of God, you will have peace in your heart. This means that when you get paid on Friday you will owe no man. How would you like to get a paycheck and owe no one? What if your grocery cabinets never went dry because every time you pulled out a can of beans, two cans came back in its place. You pulled a steak from the freezer, and God gave you two more steaks back. He restored everything back into your life. I put money into the church when I could have done something else with it. I put money in church rather than buy a car or house. I put money in church and said, "God, I prefer You over me."

God said, "There is a day I will repay you all that back. It isn't in the sweet by-and-by – it is in the nasty now-and-now." When God starts shaking it, know that it is coming your way.

On December 18 of the second year of King Darius's reign, the Lord sent this message to the prophet Haggai: This is what the Almighty Lord says! Ask the priests this question about the law. If one of you carries a holy sacrifice in his robe and happens to brush against some bread of stew or wine or oil or any other kind of food, will it also become holy?" The priests said, "No." Then Haggai asked, "If someone becomes ceremonially unclean by touching a dead person, then brushes against any of the things, will it be defiled? And the priests answered, "Yes." This is how it has been with this nation and this people, says the Lord. "Everything they do and everything they offer me has been defilet." [Haggai 2:10-14 NLT]

What would you think if God said you have not honored one thing you have given Him? Your hearts weren't right – you never thought about Him. Haggai said, "This is how it is with the people of the nations. So think about this from now on. Consider how things were going for you before you began to lay the foundation of the Lord's temple. It says, "When you hoped for a twenty bushel crop for your harvest you only got half as much – ten. When you expected fifty gallons of wine, I sent blight and mildew and hail to destroy all the products of your labor, yet even so, you refused to return to me, says the Lord."

Thank God we finally said, "God, we are going to do it." God had been speaking to us for nineteen years to do something for Him and we made up our minds we would do it. And we did it, folks!

God spoke again to the people. *"On this the 18th day of December—the day the foundation of the Lord's temple was laid—carefully consider this: I am giving you a promise now while the seed is still in the barn, before you have harvested your grain and before the grapevine, the fig tree, the pomegranate, and the olive tree have produced their crops. From this day onward I will bless you."* [Haggai 2:18-19 NLT]

In other words, God said, "It doesn't start September 24th, it didn't start on June 1st. It started on January 1st when you made a commitment to Me. From that day on, I started turning your life around. From this day forward I am shaking everything back into your life."

How would you like to get eight months of wages? Sit down and figure out how much you make a month and then multiply it by eight. What if God gave it all back to you in one month plus your September wages? God said, "While it was still in the barn I was multiplying the seeds."

From the day we started paying our property

off, from the day we made up our mind, God said He would bless us. God said, *"I will overthrow royal thrones, destroying the power of foreign kingdoms. I will overturn their chariots and charioteers. The horses will fall, and their riders will kill each other. But when this happens, says the Lord Almighty, I will honor you, Zerubbabel son of Shealtiel, my servant. I will treat you like a signet ring on my finger, says the Lord, for I have specially chosen you. I, the Lord Almighty, have spoken!"* [Haggai 2:22-23 NLT]

God said, "I have chosen this church. I have chosen you people. I have marked you and given you a sign. I want My people free. I want to use you. God said, "From that moment, I marked you — you have a mark on your hands — you can mark things."

You can read this book and it can look like something that happened thousands of years ago. Or you can bring it up to the present tense like I do and say, "God, what You did, You are still doing. All I have to do is meet the conditions of the book. That is my only responsibility. You can't plant a crop and not get a harvest out of it. God said, "I will speed up the process. You only started four or five days ago but I am going to make it look like it went back to June the 1st or January 1st when you made that commitment."

How do you make wine from water? How do you make anything? You have to be able to speed up time. Jesus speeds up time. I am 62 years old and I didn't get this far to die poor. You didn't come to this place to die poor or sick. I don't talk about wounded spirits and broken hearts. You want to write a book on hearts and sorrows? Everyone of us will get slapped sometime in our face or spit upon or talked about. What I am saying is, are we going on with God? That's the issue. Get back up – do your job!

If a husband slaps his wife, she will get angry. If he kisses her, she will get happy. If he puts a $50 bill in her hand, she will be glad. Forget about all your mistakes. Some people want to make those who hurt us suffer and be punished. We are not in the punishing business. We are in the restoration business. If the prodigal son comes home he doesn't become a slave. He comes home a son of God.

God said, "I promised you I will do it if you meet the conditions. If you do what you said and honor your words, I will take care of you." Is this your year? You have to say, "God, I have a destiny. I have overcome the devil. Satan, you have no authority over me. I will not go down – I am heading up."

Yea, though I walk through the valley of the shadow of death – in the midst of my enemies you prepare a table – you anoint my head. Surely goodness and mercy will follow me all the days of my life and I will dwell in the house of God (Psalm 23).

We break the chains of bondage, so that we can fulfill the dreams of God – whether it is to write a book, be on television, be on radio, or to go out to the four corners of this earth. We are here to reveal God's kingdom. We say to this earth, "God's kingdom has come and it is being revealed this day."

We will go forth to teach, baptize and to train in the name of Jesus. Lord, we thank You that we are saved, healed and forgiven. You said that You would shake everything for us. We allow You to begin to do that for us. Lord, we are truly the sons and daughters of God. Thank you for it in Jesus' name.

CHAPTER EIGHT

God Will Multiply Your Seed

And Jesus answered and said, Verily I say unto you, There is no man that hath left house, or brethren, or sisters, or father or mother, or wife, or children, or lands, for my sake, and the gospel's, but he shall receive an hundredfold now in this time, houses, and brethren, and sisters, and mothers, and children, and lands, with persecutions; and in the world to come eternal life. —Mark 10:29-30

If you bless others, God's blessing will come upon you. If you are willing to plant seed in the ground, God will take that seed and multiply it, provided you remain in faith and give in love. Jesus said, *It is very hard for a rich man to get into the kingdom of heaven. I say it again, it is easier for a camel to go through the eye of a needle than for a rich man to get into the kingdom of heaven.* [Matthew 19:23-24 NLT] The New Living Translation records the disciples' reaction as being *astonished* saying, *Then who in the world can ever be saved?*

I read this passage years ago and something went off inside of me thinking about the poor, just getting by disciples – why would they care if a rich person could not get into heaven? It was like they said, "Oh, my God, there is no hope for anybody then. We are following You. You are the master of the universe. You are God, and we are all rich and You are telling us that it is impossible for us rich people to get into heaven." That's what it says.

Jesus looked at them intently and said, Humanly speaking, it is impossible. But, with God, everything is possible. [Matthew 19:26 NLT] There aren't any rich people who will get saved. It is *humanly* impossible for those that have money to ever get saved.

Then Peter said, We have given up everything to follow You. What will we get out of this? You ought to be just like Peter. He wasn't interested in some sweet by-and-by. It breaks all the traditions of man to think God would want for you to live in a nice house. You think you have to build a shack for $2,000-$3,000 and live in it, but God said He would take care of you. You want to ask God, "God, if I go to church and if I serve you, and give you my life, and if I am faithful, God, what's in it for me?"

Let's see how God will reply to that. Jesus didn't scold them saying, "You bunch of demons from Hell; you are in it for the money." No, He didn't say that. Rather, He said, *I assure you that when I, the son of God sits upon the throne in the kingdom, you who have been my followers will also sit on twelve different thrones beside me and judging the tribes of Israel; and everyone who has given up houses, brothers and sisters, and fathers and mothers and children or property for my sake will receive a hundred times as much in return and shall also have eternal life.* [Matthew 19:28-29 NLT]

In other words, Jesus was saying, "I give you My word. Anything you give up for Me in the present life, I will give back to you a hundred times over, plus eternal life. I will tell you what is in it for you. I will give you more than you can spend, more than you can give away, and I will have enough left in your life that your children's children will be blessed because of you. Everybody in your family will know who you served."

How many of you who had grandparents who were drunks and whoremongers and didn't leave you a nickel? How many of you have no inheritance from your grandfathers? How many of your father's fathers left you money, land, property – lots of it and right now you can share it with us?

I bet that when Solomon died his family was

set for life. I guarantee when the Kennedys, Rockefellers, and the Bill Gates of this world die, their children's children will never have to worry about anything. Jesus said, "If you give it up to Me, I give you My word I will multiply it a hundred times what you give Me, plus I will give you eternal life."

Multiply 100 by $35,000. That's 3.5 million dollars! Let me tell you what kind of God we really serve. People will want to meet this God that said He would do all this for you.

In Luke's gospel, there was a rich man who approached the Lord, seeking what he could do to get eternal life. *Good Master, what shall I do to get eternal life? Why do you call me good, Jesus asked, only God is truly good. But as for your question, you know the commandments: Do not commit adultery. Do not murder. Do not steal. Do not testify falsely. Honor your father and mother. The man replied, I've obeyed all these commandments since I was a child. There is still one thing you lack, Jesus said. Sell all you have and give the money to the poor, and you will have treasure in heaven. Then come, follow me. When the man heard this he became sad because he was very rich. Jesus watched him go and said, How hard it is for a rich man to get into the kingdom of God.* [Luke 18: 18-24 NLT]

God is making way for you to get involved in the last days. It's like He's saying, "Come on, give up everything you have. Give it up and follow Me." I want you to know that this doesn't always mean heaven either. I know there are other ministers who have a different perspective than I, but you have to measure everything by God's word. Quit listening to men who come against what the word of God tells you.

The word of God says, "If you follow Me I will take care of you. If you follow Me it will be multiplied many, many, many times what you give up for Me. I am God. You are not God. You are a human being. I am Creator. The cattle on a thousand hills are Mine. All the gold and silver is Mine. All I want to do is release the blessings of My Son into your life."

Some of you will doubt what I'm teaching here. You will resist the truth and say, "I know you said it, but I heard this guy on television talk about it – how money is evil." Money is not evil. It is evil in the hands of people that are evil. You are not evil people. You are not losers and you need to realize this. We have had the blessings of God the whole time. What an honor it will be when these last people get connected with the blessings of God before the coming of Lord. All of a sudden the Creator pours on them in a matter of a week or month what it took you or me twenty years to accomplish. This simply proves that the word works. The last will be first. Don't get jealous. It has been yours the whole time.

The Bible teaches that you should not to let money rule over you. Don't let *it* control your life – control *it*." Folks, if you make $500.00 a week you ought to live within a budget of $500.00 a week. You don't need to try to get outside it. If you make $1,000 a week, live within it. God gave you the ability to rule your own life. If the economy ever falls, it will cost my wife and me only $300 a month to live. We don't have many expenses. If the economy folds tomorrow, I wouldn't change my lifestyle. I don't wear $500 suits. I don't live like that. If I had a million dollars I wouldn't do it. I would rather give it away and bless other people's lives. Money doesn't control me. The whole book of James deals with how you treat money – how it treats you; and in 1 Peter 5: 1-4 it talks about leadership, elders, and pastors, and overseers – they are not to be under subjection of money. You are not to be controlled by money. Leaders, you are supposed to control money. That's what makes you an elder.

It talks about deacons – those who are under the leadership of a church. If you are a deacon, you are not in the ministry to make money. That's the reason I don't take a salary. The Old Testament talks about the sheep being responsible for their shepherd. It tells you how to take care of your pastor. There is a Levitical tithe for the pastor. What you are to do is put 10% of your income into the work of God, 10% into the Levite, and 3-1/2% into the widows and orphans. You are to take care of the needy of the world. You are supposed to give 10% every three years, which comes to 30% of your income.

I am supposed to take what you give to me of that tithe, and I am supposed to tithe off the tithe. Then the Bible says that wherever you work because you give your pastor a portion of your income, God says, "If you give to your pastor a portion of what you earn at your job, then it is accounted as if the pastor was doing the work there.

Who wants to be blessed? Take care of your shepherd and then if he steals with you and doesn't tithe off the tithe, you will know because you will go bankrupt. God won't honor the preacher or the sheep. If your pastor is a God robber you will never be blessed. If he cheats and steals from God you will never be blessed.

It is time for us to rise up and become mighty men and women of God. This is what I was trying to show you. If leadership is corrupt, we have problems, folks. I hope you don't have corrupt leadership, but I am telling you if the leadership in your church is corrupt then you've got problems. Because when corrupt men lead people, the people become corrupt. You need to have Godly leadership over you—who are not in it for the money. They don't lie, cheat or steal; they give eight hours for eight hours and forty hours for forty hours. They come to work on time; they do their jobs; they walk upright before the Lord. When leadership does that, the windows of heaven are opened wide for you.

We should seek after what God wants to give us. We shouldn't want to buy what God wants to add to us. The steps of a righteous man are ordered by God. The way you treat God is the way God will treat you back. You can't stand before God one day and say, "It was the devil." The devil didn't have anything to do with it. God has given you the power to resist the devil through first submitting to the Lord (James 4:7). The devil cannot make you do anything against your will. Jesus gave you the keys to the kingdom. He said, "You have all power and all authority on heaven and on earth."

You might also say, "God allowed that to happen in my life." No, He did not. You allowed it so God had to honor *your* choice. Whatever you allow He will allow. Whatever you stop He says He will stop.

I saw a man on TV the other night who said so far he has lost $250,000 because of the stock market—in his 401(K). I don't have my money in any 401(K). God said, "Whatever you put your hand to it will prosper." (Deuteronomy 28:8) I am not going to be 65 years old and have less money than I had when I was 55 years old! God says that everything I touch will prosper. The way you give will determine how much you have to invest and contribute to other things. There are one trillion dollars that changes hands every day in America and I want to get my hands on it. I am not talking about a trillion dollars – I am talking about the blessings of God. I want to be out there tomorrow and it makes no difference what tomorrow throws at me because I know that God will take care of me. If I need a car, or a pair of pants — if I need gasoline or a hamburger, I know God will take care of me.

Have you ever had someone approach you and say, "I want to buy you a hamburger."? What if someone came up and said, "I am going to fill your car with gasoline." Wouldn't you like for that to happen everywhere you went? I am ready for the multiplication. Most people are tired of giving and getting nothing in return. I want to give and have it come back a hundred times more like the Bible promises.

This is what money is all about. The love of money is the root of all evil. That's the LOVE OF money. It is the way you treat it and respect it.

Say this prayer with me. "Father, I have been trying and giving, and the enemy has been trying and testing me. God, I will continue to give because Your word says You will give it back to me. Father, I know what today looks like but tomorrow will be different because I trust in Your promises. By the same measure that I measure, You will measure it back to me. Thank You, Jesus that I am blessed and not cursed. Amen."